THE
HOME STYLE
HANDBOOK

LUCY GOUGH

PHOTOGRAPHY BY SIMON BEVAN

MITCHELL BEAZLEY

CONTENTS

INTRODUCTION

6

PART ONE
PRINCIPLES OF HOME STYLING

12

Finding inspiration and first steps 14

•

Creating a mood board 20

•

A minimal palette 28

•

Styling basics 36

•

Creating impact in your home 54

PART TWO
THE ROOMS

112

Styling your kitchen 114

•

Styling your dining space 144

•

Styling your living room 156

•

Styling your bedroom 170

•

Styling your bathroom 180

•

Styling your home office 198

•

Styling your connecting spaces 204

A styling summary 217
Homeowners 218
Resources 219

Index 220
About the author 222
Acknowledgments 223

INTRODUCTION

When I was 14, I was given free rein to style my bedroom in whatever way I wanted and, coming from a creative family, I was allowed to go to town. I decided to splash fuchsia pink on the walls and bought a duvet cover in the same bright shade. I was given a beautiful, painted, paper Japanese parasol (a wedding favour) and hung it from my ceiling. I was also given an old, pink retro TV set from a vintage fair (it didn't work but looked fab), and I remember thinking how lucky I was to have such a beautiful room.

Now, this may sound very fancy, but in reality there was also a lot of sticky tape and blu tack (although, to my 14-year-old self, it was perfect). The room lifted my spirits every time I came home, took off my schoolbag and ran upstairs – I felt so proud of it. Little did I know that 20 years later, I would be helping other people to style their homes, so they can feel proud of their own space.

During the day, I am an Interior Stylist and Art Director who works to create exciting seasonal looks for magazines, brands and department stores. In the evenings, I run my online styling school, where I help people achieve their dream of becoming an interior stylist while also teaching others how to style their homes.

I started my online interior styling school in 2020 and soon realized that I have a passion for teaching. I love to break processes down into bite-size chunks to help people learn, and this book is an exciting extension of my courses – a natural progression if you will – and I am over the moon that you are reading it!

It is not rocket science that if you wake up in a home or room you love, which makes you feel happy and calm and brings a smile to your face, then you will start your day with a more positive mindset. And it doesn't have to cost the earth either. Paint, wallpaper, upcycling, secondhand furniture, along with a new cushion or two, can go a long way in transforming your home – and I am here to show you how.

If decorating your home were quick and easy, I would be out of a job! Restyling a home involves a lot more planning and coordination than many people realize. But I can show you how to better understand your own likes and dislikes and, hopefully, help you to decorate your home slowly while enjoying every minute of the process.

So, go ahead, make yourself a cuppa, put your feet up, and let's go on this style journey together. Lucy x

How to use this book

I have written this book as a starting point for your home-styling journey. Research is one of the most important things to do before spending money on your home. (Fun research, of course!) This can be as basic as creating a mood board or more involved with sketches and renderings. Still, either way, having some solid ideas on paper before you hire a handyman means you will have a much more successful styling outcome (and you'll save money in the process).

You can approach this book by reading it from start to finish, or you can use it as you would a deck of playing cards. You can dip in and read the pages out of order, depending on the room for which you're seeking inspiration.

Use it as a coffee table book or a reference guide for your latest home project. Mark the most important pages with large stickie notes and write your thoughts and ideas all over them. It's your book, and you should make it work for you – just as your home should work for YOU.

Don't aim for perfection in your home, or you'll be nothing but disappointed. Aim for happy, loved, soulful, interesting, beautiful and comfortable…but never ever perfect.

BEFORE WE START

I suggest you find a notebook or journal to keep all your thoughts and ideas in one place. Buy one without any ruled lines, so you can write lists and draw little sketches of items and shapes that you find along the way.

There is no better way to connect your creative thoughts than by hand. So many of us now spend less and less time putting pen to paper, opting instead for the digital format. I am guilty of doing the majority of my life admin on a computer or tablet, but when I create an interiors project from scratch, I always start with a notebook, and I keep it in my bag wherever I go.

The kind of things I like to keep notes of are costs, measurements, paint names and other bits of information that I pick up on my travels. For example, when I'm in a coffee shop, I can write down the dimensions of the pink herringbone tiles that I see on the wall. Or when I go to a friend's house, I can ask for the name of the paint colour that they've chosen for their bedroom. These are all pieces of information that come up organically in conversation and which you'll never remember six months later.

When it's time to combine your creative ideas and work on your home restyle, you can look back over all your design notes and make sense of them.

Another simple thing to do is to create a photo folder on your smartphone called 'Home Renovation'. Whenever you take a photo of something that inspires you, save it in that folder so you can access everything in one place at a later date.

These basic first steps will go a long way to helping you create a unique and individual home that you will love for years to come.

Our homes

Styling your home is about making the best use of the available space while making it look as beautiful as possible (whatever this means to you). It's not about finding the 'perfect' approach, as there are numerous ways you can style your home – just find the best use of the space for you. The home-styling journey is also about wellbeing. You want to feel good when you're at home, and your home should reflect you and your personality – aim to be surrounded by things you love.

There are two main ways to think about styling your home:

- **How it functions as a home**
- **How it looks aesthetically**

It's no good having a beautiful home if it doesn't fulfil its role practically. So, in this book, we will look at the function of every room, as that will lay the foundations for how each one should work. Then, once that information is established, you can think about the aesthetic qualities.

Daily life will feel easier when your home is working efficiently, and it's the details that count:

- Dim the lights to match the mood of the room.
- Ensure the kitchen island is at the right height for you.
- Create space for storing muddy shoes when you walk in the door.
- Check that the sides of the bath are low enough, so you don't break your back getting the kids in and out when they're little.

For me, there is nothing more exciting than restyling my home. I am always moving possessions around, so they feel new and fresh. This doesn't involve a lot of money or buying new things all the time. It's about changing things around in my home to make them work better – perhaps painting a piece of furniture to give me a hit of a new colour I love, or pairing different objects on my shelves, so they look fresh and updated.

The anticipation of how your room will look after it has been restyled is almost more exciting than reaching the outcome. Enjoy the journey while you get there!

A thank-you to the homeowners
Thank you to the 12 wonderful homeowners who opened their doors to us, so I could style beautiful rooms and magical spaces and document the process. You have been incredibly generous. Without you, this book would not have been possible. I hope you love it as much as I do.

PART ONE

PRINCIPLES OF HOME STYLING

USE YOUR HOLIDAY SNAPS
Your favourite holiday destination is
the perfect place to find inspiration for
your home. Anna and John's calm loft
bedroom (top right), painted in slubby
pinks and furnished in soft tones, looks
as if it could have been inspired by the
streets of Europe.

Finding inspiration and first steps

I am often asked, 'Where do you look for inspiration when starting a new project?' The answer is EVERYWHERE. I have always been one to stop and smell the roses (that was a criticism of one of my old managers). In fact, I remember once being asked, 'Lucy, would you stop smelling the roses and hurry up?' I didn't last long in that role...

I have always been fascinated with what I see in front of me. Whether it's the font used in a London tube station, the subtle differences in the colours of pebbles on a beach, or the colour palette used in a shopfront window – it's all there to serve as inspiration.

One thing I always do as a stylist is LOOK UP. We can be so hooked on our devices, often looking at maps or messages on our phones as we walk along. As a result, many of us fail to look above us – but there is so much to see! Architectural details, shop signs, cloud formations, neon lights and moss-covered surfaces can all feed your creative ideas when you are styling your home. You just might not know it yet!

WHERE TO FIND INSPIRATION:

Shop windows Window dressers have such a creative eye – they need to dress a tiny space for maximum impact, and I am constantly analysing how they have created their mini-masterpieces. The windows of Anthropologie are a huge favourite of mine!

Walking through a town or city with a phone/camera I take many shots of textures, surfaces and colour combinations, then save them into folders on my phone. This becomes a directory of all the things that I love.

Collections of things Walk around your home and gather trinkets you have collected over the years. Is there a colour or textural theme? Maybe you have your definitive style, after all. Use that as the springboard to your home restyle.

Florists and flower markets Have a look at the colour combinations that are put together in bouquets. There is a modern trend in floristry to use floral bunches with loose, blowsy wildflowers and foliage, and I think this is a great way to style your home too. Make the space loose, happy and relaxed. →

Nature Nature never gets it wrong! If a colour palette exists in nature, then it will work in your home. Think about the Grand Canyon or perhaps the sunflower fields in Tuscany – the colours are so harmonious within the landscape, and for this reason will always work indoors. It is just a question of identifying how you can use them in your home, which we will discuss as you navigate this book.

Look at the 'inspiration' or 'gallery' sections on home and lifestyle websites (for department stores as well as paint, fabric and wallpaper companies) Most companies hire stylists (like me) to create seasonal imagery and make their products look beautiful in real home settings. These sections of their websites are designed to help you feel inspired to create the look in your home – it's an easy win if you want to replicate the look yourself!

Hotel and restaurant bathrooms Since bathrooms are small spaces, designers often create a magical aesthetic for a WOW Instagram moment! How often do you see people taking a selfie on social media in the WC when they are out for the night? There is always a brilliant colour and tile combination going on.

SERVE IT UP
↑ Look at the tableware used in bijou restaurants and eateries. They often use high-quality cutlery and crockery with beautiful patterns and textures, and this is a great starting point for a home restyle. This beautiful crockery collection has muted tones – the perfect basis for a home colour palette.

SCULPTURAL ELEMENTS
Study the shapes in architecture, especially galleries and museums. Sculptural staircases act as the spine of the building by connecting different levels and allowing two different materials to join seamlessly.

DESIGN
AT ITS BEST
Dan and Nina's home is a masterclass of design. The pared-back palette consists of bright white, neutral textures and striking accents of blue.

There are four points that we will talk a lot about in this book. I call them the PREP formula.

Palette
Repetition
Edit
Place

Palette

It's important to decide on a colour palette and to STICK TO IT. It's the number one rule. Choose your colours (use only three, four or five) and repeat them throughout your home. You can use them in different proportions and in different ways in each room (for example, a caramel wall in the living room, a caramel bathmat in the bathroom and a caramel bedhead in the bedroom), but stick to the colours.

Repetition

This is intertwined with Palette, but you need to repeat the theme/trend/colour/thread throughout your home. It's how you keep your ideas edited down and create a sense of cohesion. Stay consistent with your materials, colours, plants and general styling ideas in each room. For example, Dan and Nina used vertical wooden panels in many rooms – some painted, some not – but they make a wonderful, contemporary thread.

Edit

All the homes we covet are edited and sorted out, and the clutter has been minimized. I am not saying that you can't own many things, just that they all need to work together and sit within your mood board. Yes, this will mean you need to have a clear-out!

Place

Everything should have a place in your home. This entails giving your objects and furniture some space, so they are not on top of each other. This is linked to the Edit step. When you look in your cupboards, everything should have a place and not be jammed in with everything else. This will help when tidying up, as you'll know where everything needs to go at the end of the day, which means only owning functional, beautiful or timeless items. It can take a while to achieve this goal – but this is a long game and doesn't have to happen overnight.

CREATING
A MOOD BOARD

⬤

Let's start at the very beginning . . . mood boards are the origin of all well-styled spaces. Ask any interior designer or stylist, and they will tell you that every project begins with a mood board. Little bits of fabric and wallpaper glued onto a piece of A3 cardboard may seem like a waste of time, but trust me, it is a very important step! If you're like me and you have a very busy, creative mind, you'll need to concentrate all your creative thoughts in one place, so they start to form a cohesive idea. I would argue that most people own a hotchpotch collection of things at home, consisting of hand-me-downs, heirlooms, eBay finds, IKEA pieces, with some expensive items thrown in too. But when it comes to styling a dream space, you need to consider which items to keep and which to give away or replace.

If you create a mood board, then it will give you a basic understanding of your colour palette and favourite textures, as well as an overall feel for the room, so you can start your new space afresh. Fill your mood board with a variety of colours, textures, patterns and found objects, as well as printed images of furniture, fabrics, wallpapers, paints, surfaces, fixtures and accessories.

With a mood board, you are creating a micro-world that can be enlarged and exploded in a room or even your whole house – depending on the size of your project.

Ideally, this planning stage will be fairly detailed. The more thorough you are with the planning, the fewer mistakes you will make and the less money you'll end up spending on the wrong things!

1: Build it up

Build up your mood board, starting with the largest pieces at the bottom and working your way up to create a beautifully tonal palette.

TOP TIP
Create more than one mood board when you start your research, as you might find that you prefer multiple aesthetics. Then narrow it down to your favourite after that.

The best mood board will feature a mixture of the following:

- Paint (use a tester pot on some paper or a paint swatch) and include a maximum of five colours
- Wallpaper sample(s)
- Fabric sample(s)
- One or more curvy, shapely objects

- Some foliage or a flower, even it is just a single stem or leaf – always try to reflect nature in your home
- Something textural
- A few of the trinkets that you love

2: Collect things

Collect various items from around your home. Find things that you love in one colour palette (for example, the mood board opposite is multiple shades of green, brick, pale woods and pale pink), which will fit on an A3 piece of paper.

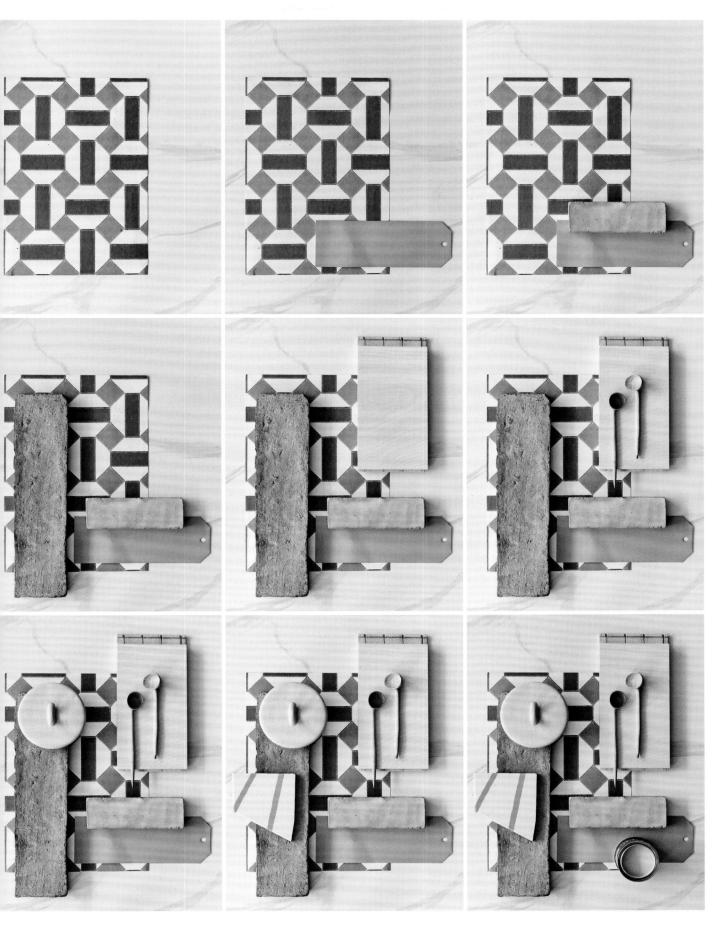

3: Organize items

Organize the items on your mood board in an orderly fashion. Don't overcrowd the items, giving them space to breathe and keeping things neat and tidy.

Overlap items on your mood board and think about ratios: the more you see of one item, the more you would represent that in your room scheme.

Always use at least one organic item – perhaps a leaf, a flower stem or some foliage – and remember to stick to your chosen colour palette.

4: Enjoy it!

Make sure you don't take the process too seriously – a mood board is all about enjoying your first step into a scheme that feels unique and entirely YOU.

You could go 'shopping' for the items listed here. Online is a good place to start. Here are some example terms (which were used to create the two boards opposite) that you can explore using Pinterest, hashtags, search engines and online shop search functions:

ONE BOARD, INFINITE OUTCOMES

← Here are two finished rooms that could be the outcome of the mood boards shown above them. The room on the left is in a city home and the image on the right was taken in a country home. Both have similar textures, tones and surfaces, but these are used in two different ways. The city home feels modern because the surfaces are smooth, while the one on the right feels rustic since the textures are more organic. It's the same palette taken in two different directions.

- Earthenware
- Birch plywood
- Concrete
- Monochrome
- Rustic timber
- Dried flowers
- Chalky grey
- Ditsy floral
- Arts & Crafts patterns
- Dark brown
- Muted silver tones
- Abstract art
- Pale timbers
- Off-white marble
- Stone
- Bentwood

5: Break it down

Now, you might be thinking, 'How can I translate my mood board into my home? It's just a bunch of stuff!' Well, let's break this down to make things easier. Take a look at the image on the right.

- The soft blue paint could be used as paint in the space, but it could also become the colour of your fabric sofa, the kitchen cabinets or the rubber flooring in your bathroom.
- The white string could translate into textured tiles for a splashback.
- The pipe could become plaster corbels around the walls of your home or inspire some shabby chic furniture.
- The pretty safety pin card could be used as inspiration for artwork or wallpaper in your bedroom or perhaps a set of Delft pottery tableware stored on open shelves in the kitchen.
- The lacy fabric could become a tablecloth, bedding, curtains or cushions.

See where I am going with this? Your mood board is the start of a million possibilities. No single idea is best – it is simply one of the choices you could make. But rest assured that if everything you source and buy sits within the parameters of this scheme, it will feel like a very well-thought-out and beautifully designed home.

TO GET YOU STARTED
Place your items in the gridlines shown opposite. Put the circular items in the circles, the square shapes in the squares, and the foliage on the leaves. Move things around, keep everything straight and parallel, and remember always to have some fun!

A MINIMAL PALETTE

A small palette of colours and textures is the key to every successful space – it unites a home and will be the main thread throughout this book. The number one guiding principle in all home projects is to keep the colour and texture palette minimal. Five to six colours and textures are the ultimate number to aim for. It should never be only about the colours – when gathering samples for your palette, I suggest incorporating one or two textures and surfaces too. I would include surfaces like wood, brick or ceramics in your palette of five or six. I don't like laying down hard-and-fast rules when it comes to home styling, but I believe this to be the ONE CORE RULE.

Use colour as the thread in your home

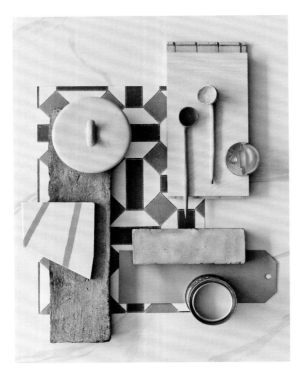

A dream interior surrounds you with colours that make you smile. However, too many colours can feel overwhelming and visually confusing. Here, India has used a dream palette of six main colours and textures throughout her family home. She has an excellent eye for detail and a fantastic sense of colour – her home is a real feast for the eyes. India's colour palette consists of:

- Pale brick
- Farrow & Ball's Pink Ground
- Verdant green
- White marble
- Brass
- Golden brown materials like rattan and oak

CONNECT THE SPACE
The palette has been used throughout India and Tom's home, so every room feels connected. The colours (mainly soft pink, green and marble) feature in different quantities, which means each room has its own personality – all the while sticking to a single mood board.

TOP TIP
You can paint a cast-iron bath to match the colour scheme in your bathroom. There is more information on this on page 192.

A MINIMAL PALETTE

Primary, secondary and accent colours

If you'd like to see what your three main colours – primary, secondary and accent – will look like together in a room, then grab some paint swatches (you can either get these from a local DIY store or paint cardboard with tester pots). Now layer the three colours on the rectangles opposite.

- The primary colour is the main one that you will use on the walls of the room, and this should be placed on the red rectangle.
- The secondary colour is the colour that you plan to use on other large surfaces in the room – the floor or cupboard doors, for example, or the ceiling or bedspread (note that a bed counts as a large surface area).
- The accent colour is the one you might use for smaller accent spots such as cushions, window trims, a chair or anywhere you wish to add a smaller pop of colour (or white).
- This process will give you a good idea of the ratio of the different colours in the room when your project is complete.

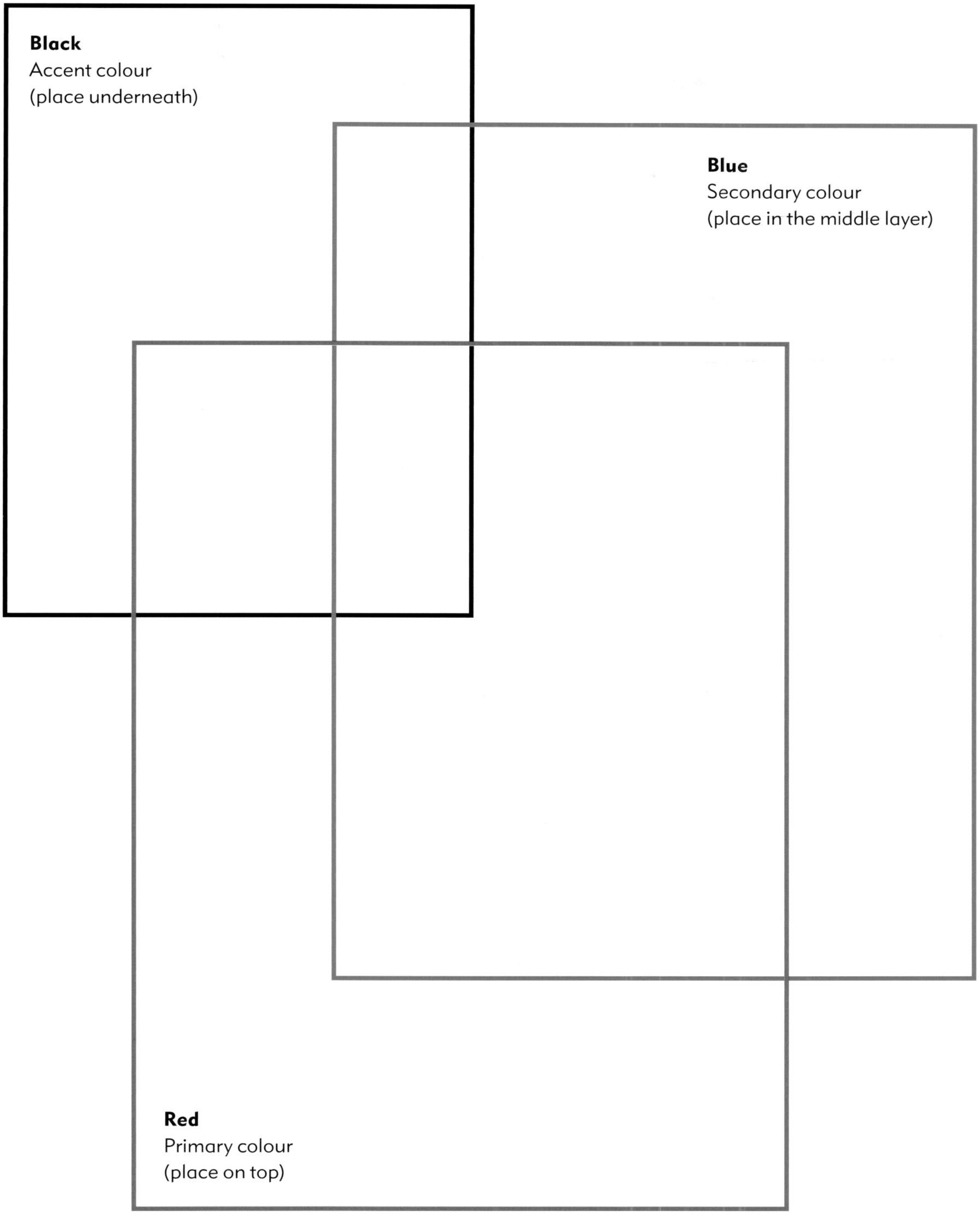

Black
Accent colour
(place underneath)

Blue
Secondary colour
(place in the middle layer)

Red
Primary colour
(place on top)

Using a dark palette

You'll love this scheme if you prefer a darker palette for your home. Claire from Louisa Grace interiors has an incredible way of layering dark on dark in her own home and curating vintage items that she sources from near and far.

If you would like to replicate this atmospheric scheme, then your starting point for a mood board could be your 'favourite thing' – perhaps a vintage key from your great-grandparents' home or an old photo of the street you grew up in.

Then add colours that you love and treasures from around your home, and bring these together with surface samples and foliage. If you decide to go with two or more bold colours, add some soft tones in between to give them space to breathe.

Once you are happy with your palette, you can start shopping and sourcing gorgeous items for your home. Claire has stuck to a minimal palette for her maximalist home, using the colour green, aged timber, lots of foliage and vintage wonders.

SEARCH FOR TREASURES
↑ Look around your home and take note of the treasured things you own. Chances are a colour palette will emerge that you can turn into a whole room scheme. This beautiful home uses a palette of muddy colours, tactile surfaces and eclectic treasures.

CONTINUITY IS KEY
↑ Continue the palette throughout the rest of your home, keeping with the same colours, textures, treasures and foliage and using them on repeat.

STYLING
BASICS

Not to be confused with an interior decorator or interior designer, an interior stylist will change your home's aesthetic character, including the furniture, walls, flooring, lighting and accessories, so it reflects you and your personality. In this chapter, I show you how to style horizontal surfaces and create still-life moments, sharing the basic techniques I use every day. Not only can styling shelves, cabinets and dressers make a room look pleasing, it can also be a mindful task – I love shuffling objects, stacking books and layering items. With careful curation this styling can be inexpensive but make a huge difference to the look of a room. Also, as there's no structural work, it doesn't matter if you're renting – it's about the temporary elements you add and how you arrange them. Don't forget: the key to a well-styled space is to make it feel natural and UN-styled – it should be effortless and unforced.

How to style shelves

When styling shelves, I like to start with an object that I feel has enough weight and height to anchor the display. Then I will style everything else in relation to that object.

1. For a setup such as this, I always clear everything away so I can start with a blank space. If you look at the last image (6), you will see it has been planned around a diagonal line – there is a vague visual line running from bottom left to top right, which helps the display to feel more curated.

2. Find your focal object with good weight and height – in this case, the vase of flowers – and position it to the right of the diagonal.

3. Keep the weight of the display to the right as you add other substantial objects such as this horned ornament, but maintain some balance to the left – here, this is achieved with a shallow wooden bowl.

4. & 5. Continue adding other objects to complement the key ones, using something old, something new, something textured and something organic. Keep to a minimal colour palette for a contemporary, timeless feel.

6. As you add the last pieces, stick to the tonal colour palette – this collection is a mix of browns and grey with a hint of soft pink. Including a soft pink neon light helps to make the space feel contemporary.

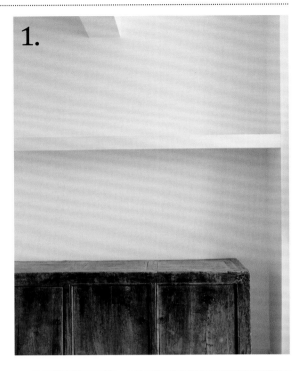

1.

4.

When styling a pared-back, grown-up bookcase in an alcove such as this, it always helps to have a strong base colour as the foundation of the room. Here, India has chosen a beautiful shade of green for her living room walls, shelves, fireplace and cabinetry. I always applaud people for using strong colours. It rarely goes wrong, although a lot of people might be apprehensive about splashing such a deep colour on their walls. But look how gorgeous this looks! Here are the key styling points for achieving this display:

1. Remove all the items from the shelves and start with a blank slate.

2. & 3. After deciding on an asymmetrical approach, I added a plant next and put books horizontally and vertically in six little stacks.

4. & 5. I then placed the shell vase to act as an anchor before adding the remainder of the objects. An uneven number of objects is always the best formula, so aim for three, five, seven or nine items, and so on. Every shelf is split 50/50 between dark and light objects.

6. All the objects in the display are roughly in the same colour palette.

TOP TIP
Remember that if there is a trusty source of natural light in the room, the room won't feel dark and poky.

TOP TIP
Aim to start with the tallest things at the back, then choose objects that gradually become smaller as you move to the front.

A CURATED COLOUR PALETTE

↑ Jessie has hung a hand-stitched fabric wall hanging (which she created herself – @cuttsandsons) above a beautiful collection of treasures. The colours of the artwork, the wall paint and the objects on the sideboard are all perfectly curated from the same rich, earthy palette. Visually it helps to have all the objects sitting at different heights, as you can see here.

POCKETS OF COLOUR

→ Jessie is a master at arranging her treasures and has a wonderful cabinet with each section styled as a colour block of curiosities. I find that when you have guests over, they are always drawn to your treasures during quiet moments. They are such lovely conversation starters.

Frame with foliage

Using foliage to frame a bookcase or set of shelves is a favourite styling tip of mine. Thanks to the resurgence in popularity of houseplants over the last few years, there is now an abundance of plants to choose from at every DIY store, gift shop and flower market.

PLANTS AND PAINT

→ Trailing plants look fabulous hanging down one side of a bookshelf to soften it, as here in India's home. This soft sage-green cabinet provides a calming base colour for the scene.

Shelf styling takeaways

- I have drawn triangles over the image above to show how I use a triangular formation when positioning items on shelves. This helps to keep things feeling informal but still curated.
- Find your hero vessels, plates and candles, then place them in triangular formations.
- Create a sense of depth by placing objects in front of each other.
- Aim to include items with different heights to keep the display feeling relaxed.
- Stick to a gorgeous, minimal colour palette.
- Placing a small object at the base of the display at the front is like placing a full-stop at the end of a sentence.
- Plants in front of objects can make beautiful shadows and brighter spots. Start with a trailing plant to create this effect.

Make the display tonal

There are several core principles at play in this three-shelf display:

- The backdrop is a tonal, textural wall covering. Texture helps to make the display visually exciting.
- The shelf has been styled using the triangle method (see page 44) – draw visual lines between the organic plant vessels and you can see the three-sided shape.
- A minimal colour palette of earthy, natural colours is used.
- The display contains a mix of natural shapes and straight-edged items.
- Everything has breathing space with none of the items being too close together.

A SINGLE COLOUR PALETTE

← Dan and Nina's 'shelfie' is a beautiful lesson in using a single colour palette on shelving. The beautiful brown and terracotta shades with a touch of black are absolute perfection.

The perfect shelf formula

If you are arranging a single shelf, then explore these ideas:

- Place the tallest item on the left and the shorter items to the right of the shelf. Bingo!
- Using just two or three colours is perfect.
- Position the shelf so it's level with your eyeline, ensuring that it isn't too high or too low on the wall.
- Organic shapes (meaning they don't have any sharp edges) look beautiful when they are grouped together.
- Including one or more plants is always to be encouraged.

RULES FOR STYLING

→ You could draw a diagonal line above Jessie's shelf from the pleated table lamp (the tallest item) on the left to the red jug placed on the right. Everything in between gradually descends in height. The framed painting is by Frankie Thorp.

DIAGONAL SIGHTLINE

There needs to be something in your eyeline (the place where the eye lands when you are looking straight ahead), whether it is a painting or a plant. In this image, the top of the plant on the left is in your eyeline. Visually, it helps your eye to land on something in the top left of the space and to look diagonally down to the right. This preference is because in Western culture our brains have been trained to read from top left to bottom right.

THE PERFECT VIGNETTE

↑ The home of Noel and Matt includes this beautiful conservatory at the back of the house. Outside the window is a bamboo garden that presses against the frosted glass and gives the feeling of living in a greenhouse.

It's a beautiful, serene space to pass through as you walk from one side of the house to the other. Notice how the objects and plants on the cabinet are higher in the top left and then go down at an angle to the bottom right.

How to style still-life moments

Use your camera

Think of your home as a series of vignettes. When you are trying to style a specific section of a room, get your camera out and think about the space as a photograph. This gives you boundaries to work within and enables you to compartmentalize a room into a series of smaller spaces.

Make it tactile

It can make a big difference if you style every corner of your home as beautifully as you can, so it becomes a destination in itself – secondary spaces don't need to be an afterthought of the main design. Use tactile objects in your vignette to make you want to walk over and pick them up.

STYLE A VIGNETTE

← Everywhere you turn in Dan and Nina's house there is a ready-made vignette. The same principles apply here as they do when styling a simple shelf. You can see that furniture placement began with the tallest item on the left (the potted tree) and the shortest on the right (the small wooden stool). And Maisey, Dan and Nina's dog, ties in beautifully too!

THINK LIKE AN ARTIST

→ Christabel's choice of putty-coloured wall paint and a traditional side table makes this corner of her home feel like a painting by a Dutch master.

This mirror and wooden side table fit perfectly in the quirkily shaped space. Take measurements of areas such as these and keep them on your phone for when you are out shopping. You may just find the perfect items for the space.

IT'S ALL ABOUT BALANCE

Balancing out the hard and soft items in a vignette is important. Dried foliage (like this pampas grass) has a lovely colour and soft texture, and is always a talking point (if you know, you know!). This beautiful corner of Claire and Jamie's home is the perfect pairing of vintage and contemporary, hard and soft, dark and light, while keeping to a minimal, tonal colour palette.

ADD VELVET TO YOUR PALETTE

Reupholstering your sofa using a rich, velvet fabric is guaranteed to bring a little bit of magic to a room. Light falls beautifully on velvet, and it's hard-wearing and ages well too. Re-covering furniture is also a great way to keep an existing sofa, even if you decide to restyle the rest of the room using a new colour palette. If you're ever unsure which colour of velvet to use, take a leaf out of Claire McFadyen's book and match your sofa to your dog!

CREATING IMPACT
IN YOUR HOME

When restyling a home, I like to create a WOW factor on entering the rooms. Whether you use paint, an artwork or a mural, an unusual piece of furniture or a large bunch of flowers, something out of the ordinary always turns heads. Colour is one of the easiest and most cost-effective ways to create a show-stopping space, and it's possible to paint an amazing, mood-enhancing room for very little money. You could display a large piece of art or a large mirror (look in secondhand stores for inexpensive items), or even paint your own artwork! For a calmer space, I prefer to use a few large items instead of lots of small objects. I like to draw the eye down the room to something large and unusual to pique the interest and use groups of objects to tell a story. This chapter shows how to create breathtaking moments in your home and will hopefully give you the confidence to try these ideas yourself.

My quick tips for a beautiful home

Style loosely. Linen cushions, for example, look good even when they are crumpled.

Use personal objects that you absolutely love. Make use of your 'best' things every day – don't save them just for special occasions.

Use a variety of items in a room, including good-quality objects, heirlooms, quirky knick-knacks, found objects and, most of all, things that make you feel happy when you look at them.

Keep things tidy but comfortable. Perfection is not the aim when you are styling your home.

Mix traditional and contemporary furniture to help your home appear timeless. For instance, your grandmother's Singer sewing machine table would look amazing with a modern print above it.

Use a similar colour palette for everything in your home. I always stick to just a few colours.

Always use real foliage and flowers in your home, especially cuttings from your garden – make sure you leave enough outside for the bees and butterflies.

Decorating with colour

Using colour in your home is one of the most transformative things you can do to a space. There are a few principles to bear in mind, however. Too many colours will make your home feel overwhelming and fussy, but if you stick to just a small selection, it will feel calm, considered and chic. Use colours that inspire you and make you feel happy and positive by all means, but also consider the function of the room. For example, bright colours are great for an area where you want to feel energized, while calm and muted tones are ideal for a bedroom or an office space.

The power of one

Stunning colour alert! Painting one block of colour on every surface, including the walls and window trim, is a great way to turn heads. The picture on the right is one of my favourite rooms featured in the book. Here, Farrow & Ball's rich and buttery India Yellow adorns every surface, helping to make the space feel warm and inviting. Thankfully, because the small room has a decent natural light source, the colour doesn't make it feel dark.

PRIVACY MATTERS
→ Matt chose contemporary ribbed glass for the lower half of this bathroom window for added privacy. This alleviates the need for a curtain and allows light to stream in all day.

TOP TIP
Matching furniture, fixtures and accessories to the colour of the wall can also create a WOW moment in a room – especially those items that lie flat against the wall, such as radiators and bedheads.

Choose a calm colour for extra Zen. A soft tone such as a sage or mint colour is very calming for the eyes – perfect for a high-energy room like Jessie's playroom. Furthermore, pink and green are a classic match – pink helps to warm the green, while the green helps to ground the pink.

Decorative finishes – DIY

Paint is one of the most versatile things you can use to transform your home. If you have a little time and would like to try out some new DIY skills, you can create something beautiful for a small amount of money.

LEARN NEW SKILLS

↑ Christabel painted dark and light blue diamonds on her fireplace hearth in chalky, historic colours to add some interesting detail. If you're like me and scared to paint anything too fiddly, opting for a solid shape with straight edges, like a diamond, provides the perfect starting point.

Steps to success:

1. Clean back the surface using an old rag and some degreasing product.
2. Cut washing-up sponges into diamond shapes.
3. Dip the sponges into your chosen chalk paint (try Annie Sloan Chalk Paint®) and dab in a grid fashion to create a beautiful pattern.

KIDS LOVE COLOUR
← John and Anna have succeeded in making a feature out of a quirky old cupboard in a kid's bedroom by painting the room in a jewel-like colour palette. Kids love bright, happy colours, so why not go to town?

TOP TIP
You may be thinking, 'I would never be bold enough to paint my room that colour. How do I know it will work?' But remember to consult nature – this palette exists on your local nature walk.

Colour in the conservatory

Conservatories are often white, but this bright, happy example in the perfect shade of mint green helps to create a more interesting space than the average white structure.

If you want a coloured conservatory, you have two options. You can talk to the conservatory company before installation to see if they can manufacture it in your favourite colour before it arrives. Or you might want to paint the conservatory after installation. In that case, you need to choose the right paint, as conservatories tend to be very sunny (hence why they are sometimes called sunrooms), and any paint will fade faster than in other rooms in the house. For a topcoat, look for solar-reflective and anti-glare paint. And most definitely use an all-surface primer for the undercoat. The best option is to seek the advice of a painter and decorator or to call a local conservatory company and ask their professional opinion before starting to paint.

Mix and match colourful patterns

A note on matching patterns. Surprise, surprise!
It's all about the colour palette... If you have two
or three patterns in a room and are unsure how to
coordinate them, then stick to a thread of colour
throughout the different patterns.

A PURPLE THREAD
← The light purple tiles
and the armchair tie in
unexpectedly because
they are the same shade.

A PINK THREAD
→ Pink-striped wallpaper
and a pink-patterned
sofa in Caroline's
loft bedroom work
beautifully together here
because they share a
colour thread.

Paint

Which paint to use

- Primer: To seal and protect bare surfaces that have never been painted before.
- Undercoat: This protects surfaces and also prevents existing paint from coming through the topcoat. Try to match dark paint with a dark undercoat, and light paint with a light undercoat.
- Walls and ceilings: Here, you mainly need emulsion paints. (Emulsion is basically your standard wall paint.) Emulsion has either acrylic or vinyl added for durability and to make painted surfaces more hard-wearing.
- Wood and trim: Shop the eggshell range, or use gloss if you want a shiny finish.
- Brick and external: For these, you'll need masonry paint and external wood paint.
- Furniture: Opt here for chalk paint or gloss paint.

Paint finishes

- Matte and flat matte: Have a non-shiny, matte appearance.
- Satin: Has a light sheen and is mainly used on woodwork.
- Silk: Has a light sheen and is for walls and ceilings – especially in kitchens and bathrooms, as it is wipeable.
- Chalk: A paint that produces a chalky, matte finish. It is more eco-friendly, as it doesn't contain acrylic or oils. Can be used on most surfaces.
- Gloss: Ideal for a high-shine effect. Perfect for woodwork but can also be used on walls if you are feeling adventurous.

Note: The above is just a guide – always check the paint tin before buying to ensure you have the right paint for the surface.

How much wall paint do you need for the average room?

- Typical feature wall: 2 litres (½ gallon)
- Small room (3 × 3m/10 × 10ft): 4 litres (1 gallon)
- Large room (6 × 6m/20 × 20ft): 8 litres (2 gallons)

Shopping list for the DIY store (take a photo of this page with you!)

- The name and brand of your chosen paint (if you have already decided on this).
- Undercoat, if required – always use this if you are painting a lighter paint over a dark colour or if you are painting a wall that has never been painted before. It's more effective to paint a decent undercoat than to attempt multiple topcoats.
- Masking tape (FrogTape® is my personal favourite).
- White vinegar to clean off mould.
- Sandpaper to smooth back raised areas that you have filled with Polyfilla.
- Paint roller pole.
- Roller sleeve and frame (one for each paint colour).
- Angled paintbrush for cutting in.
- Paintbrush.
- Bucket and sponge.
- Ladder or kick-step.
- Scraper.
- Sealant.

1.

Dark ceiling, white walls. Matt's statement green ceiling is a favourite design feature of mine. It's like putting a 'hat' on your room. Painting a colour above a picture rail helps to draw the eye upward and will make the room look taller.

We spend so many hours in our homes that how they look can have a real impact on our mental health. For this reason, creating a space that reflects our personality and values is very important. One of the easiest and most cost-effective ways to transform a space is by painting the walls, trims, floors and ceilings. In this section of the book, I will show you four beautiful ways to paint a room, which are sure to bring a timeless quality to your home.

2.

Match the ceiling colour to the wall colour, as Jessie has here. It pays to choose a fairly light tone in a hard-working communal space like a living room. The room could feel like a cave if it's too dark and the natural light isn't strong enough, so this effect is best for those with a decent-sized window. Painting the ceiling and walls in the same pale shade gives the room depth and interest but doesn't make it feel dark and poky. The painting in the alcove is by Chris McKimmie.

3.

Paint the walls and ceiling in two different colours to sit side by side, as with the soft pink panelling and olive-green ceiling of this cosy bedroom. The muted green allows the slubby pink to stand out and both colours work in harmony. The soft colour of the contemporary tongue-and-groove panels paired with the traditional bedhead feels timeless, and the image could have been shot in 1922 or 2022 – that's the beauty of good design.

OPTICAL ILLUSIONS

If you want a room to look narrower, paint the two side walls a darker colour, so they feel closer to you.

If you want a room to look longer, paint the wall furthest away in a light and bright colour, so you look ahead to it.

If you want a room to feel bigger, stick with lighter colours.

4.

Use exposed plaster, a look
that is becoming increasingly
popular. Just leave freshly exposed
plaster on the walls and ceiling, as Jessie
has, while stripping back the paint from
the window surrounds and leaving them
raw. Here, the warmth of the smooth
plaster is bathed in soft light from the
window overlooking the harbour –
it creates a beautiful effect.

Textured walls

Dan and Nina's master bedroom is covered in textured Venetian plaster – a luxurious and bespoke wall treatment. The plaster is made of a thin veneer of slaked lime putty (made from limestone and water). The way the light falls on plaster walls is infinitely more beautiful than the light falling on a flat matte paint, due to the organic, traditional nature of the material and how it's applied. Bauwerk limewash paint, chalk wall paint, exposed plaster, microcement and tadelakt are all variations of textured wall finishes that you can use to achieve a similar effect.

Think about window trims

Should you match the window trims to the walls or make them clash? This is a question of personal taste, but bear in mind that a room will look larger if you have a lighter-coloured window trim, as in the room on the left. If you paint the trim in a dark colour, the window will stand out and appear closer to you, making the room seem a bit smaller, as in the room below with artwork on the wall by Kate Black. This is great if you have a very large room and want to help it feel cosier. Painting window trims can be a great way to give them a new lease of life and add some design flair to a space. It's also something you could do yourself as a weekend update.

UPVC WINDOWS

Many of us will inherit white UPVC/plastic windows when we move into a new home and, sadly, these are not so easy on the eye. However, the good news is, you can paint them! Here's how:

- Clean the windows, getting rid of any cobwebs (and salt if you live near the sea).
- Cover the edges of the glass with some masking tape (to avoid painting the glass as well).
- Use an all-surface primer as the undercoat first.
- Choose a suitable paint that will bond to the window trim – try an all-purpose exterior eggshell or a gloss paint. Also apply two decent coats of paint.

Painting with white

White is probably the most popular surface finish by a long mile. It is versatile and neutral, and many people choose to have a white backdrop and then add colour to the room through their furniture and accessories.

Sadly, there is no one perfect white paint. You will have to test a few shades of white on your walls to find the right one for you. But here are some guidelines to help you on your way.

When shopping for whites, it is handy to have a brilliant white paint swatch in your notebook (make sure this is a clean one with no smudges). Carry this around with you, so you can compare whites to it. Warmer whites will have a pinky-reddy tone (subtly, of course), while colder whites will have more of a blue-grey tint.

TOP TIPS
If your home is modern and has strong architectural features, consider using cooler whites.

If your home is an older, period-style property, then warmer whites will be the best shade for you.

Some reasons why people love white paint:

- White is timeless.
- It's a classic choice and never goes out of style.
- Easy to source.
- It can feel like a fresh start.
- Perfect for homes in hotter climates because it feels cool.
- Wonderful in small, poky homes that need brightening up.
- Usually the least expensive paint in the range.
- It's a calm and meditative colour.
- Considered a suitable colour for minimalist schemes, which have become very popular over the last few years.
- There are thousands of shades to choose from (although this can make it difficult to choose).

Styling with neutrals

Now, let's talk about the tricks to use when styling with neutrals, as these two very valid questions come up repeatedly with my online students:

- My home is all white – is that boring?
- How do I style my white or neutral home?

First, there is nothing wrong with choosing white-on-white as a home scheme. White/cream is probably the most popular way to style one's home, as it feels bright, fresh and clean.

In places like Australia, South Africa and California, where there is plenty of daylight all year round, it makes sense to use a white palette, as it helps to make the house feel cool on a hot day.

Generic white paint is the least expensive on the market, and white furniture is widely available in most stores, so people often think, 'If I do it all in white, I can't go wrong.' However, the one golden rule to making a white home feel exciting is the need to incorporate TEXTURE. Using texture (and more texture!) will give a space depth, interest and more contrast than if you just choose flat white for everything.

Texture swap:
- Change cotton bedding to linen.
- Place a linen slipcover over your existing sofa.
- Use textured white wallpaper on walls (Anaglypta wallpaper is fabulous and you can paint it in any neutral shade you want). More contemporary patterns have been added to the range in the last few years – they are no longer classified as granny-chic!
- Choose cushion covers with a chunky weave or that are stitched with embroidery.
- Replace cheap white IKEA furniture with secondhand quality timber that you can paint white and still see some wooden texture coming through. Annie Sloan's white chalk paint is fabulous for painting on any surface without the need to apply an undercoat first.
- Choose off-white and pale putty-coloured paints instead of stark white in order to warm up a room.

Texture is key
→ Dan and Nina's textured living room wall has a smooth finish and yet it also has depth because of the layered effect. Light falls beautifully on this wall, which has a more organic appearance than flat matte paint.

BUY PRELOVED DOORS

Salvage yards have hundreds of doors in different sizes, and while you may need a bit of patience to source the exact size you need, it shouldn't be too difficult to find a door that you can retrofit to the doorway.

Buying preloved items

I have always loved styling a home with a selection of vintage pieces. Or at least with a mix of vintage and new items. I believe that the essence of a timeless interior (the type of interior I strive for in every project) is to combine items from the past and the present.

Vintage is important for so many reasons. One is the energy that vintage items hold. A beautiful piece of vintage furniture is like a hug. It's warm to the touch, tactile when you run your hand over it, and it often smells as if it has had a life – it is far removed from the mixture of MDF and wood glue found in so many inexpensive new pieces on the high street. Think about the following:

- If you can buy/find/save a secondhand piece, then you have kept it out of landfill – something we all need to be more conscious of.
- A preloved item adds character to a home and helps inspire conversation. It also makes a home feel well considered. I am not fond of homes where all the items look as if they have been bought from the same shop – I like spaces with more soul than that.
- If you buy a piece of preloved furniture, it can give you an interesting project to work on. You might need to sand it back, repaint it, wax it, and so on. I love using my hands when I am being creative – the satisfaction of the finished product can be joyous.
- A preloved item often tells an interesting story. I bought an old blanket box years ago with the address of a soldier painted on the top. I researched who he was, and it turns out he lived close to where one of our relatives lived. The world is much smaller than we realize, and I love being able to tell people where an item came from and what it was used for.

MY QUICK TIPS FOR BUYING THE BEST SECONDHAND FURNITURE

- Look for woodworm holes (these are tiny holes with a fine powdery dust around them) and avoid purchasing those pieces at all costs.
- Sit on sofas and chairs, open up cupboards and lean on tables – this will help you identify whether a piece is sturdy or needs structural work.
- Always confirm that all parts are accounted for.
- Sniff a sofa. If it smells musty, it may have internal mould.
- Check the upholstery fabric – does it need replacing? If it is a well-known brand, you might be able to buy a new slipcover for it.
- Look past chipped paint. Surface damage is fine, as you can easily respray or repaint the item. Just look carefully for any structural damage.
- If surface discoloration occurs on a metal item, then you could always respray it.

How to de-orange wooden furniture
Orange wooden furniture is less pleasing to the eye than the more contemporary blonde woods. But a lot of secondhand furniture on the market is the colour of a sweet potato! One of my favourite ways to de-orange wooden furniture is to strip off the existing layer of varnish with some paint stripper. I then coat the wood with clear furniture wax and work this in. When dry, it will have a natural finish without the orange.

Matching art to your home

How to choose and display art

Choosing and hanging art in your home is one of the final pieces of the decorating puzzle. Embellish your walls as you would add jewellery to an outfit – it helps to add some WOW to your home! There are two main factors to think about:

1. You must fall in love with the artwork and it must stir up emotion when you look at it. Don't worry about whether other people like it – you are the one who has to look at it every day.
2. The artwork needs to fit into the colour palette of the room where it will hang.

Use a laser for accurate hanging

If you are not a fan of picture rails, then you will need to make holes in your walls in order to hang pieces of art. Consider using an electric laser level to ensure you hang an artwork straight. I like to hang pictures just above my eyeline, so I don't have to look up too much to see them.

Art is portable

Remember, art is portable and can be repositioned as many times as you like. One of my greatest pleasures is moving things around in my home periodically, so the room schemes always feel fresh and different.

Key points to consider:

1. How big is your space/wall? Always buy the biggest piece of art you can afford for the space. A larger print or original piece will look better than a small one floating in a big space.
2. Do you already own some suitable art or will you buy something especially for the wall? If you own the artwork, consider changing the frame to suit the space. If you want to buy art, this is the perfect chance to buy something in the perfect colour palette for the room. Stick to your house mood board to make sure the colours will work together.
3. Are the walls rendered brick or plaster? If you have plaster walls, you can use a soft wall hanging kit and easily tap in hooks to support the artwork. If you have hard walls, you will need a drill with a masonry bit attachment to drill through the brick behind. You will also need wall plugs to ensure the screws stay in place in the wall.

COLOUR HIGHLIGHT
→ The verdant green landscape featured in this vintage artwork matches the rich green window frame at the foot of Jessie's staircase.

**BUY ART TO
SUIT YOUR HOME**
Jessie is a master of colour
coordination. Burnt orange, dark
marble, maroon and creams make for
a beautiful, sophisticated colour palette.
The artwork on display fits perfectly into
this colour scheme. The contemporary
feel of the artwork by indigenous
Australian artist Judy Martin
helps to make the vignette
feel timeless.

Use picture rails

Install a picture rail high up around the perimeter of a room. That way, you can display art wherever you wish and hang it at the desired height by adjusting the string length. It is also easier to move art around without putting holes in the walls.

MAKE A CHOICE
↑ Choosing an artwork that matches the wall colour (or a wall colour that matches your favourite art), like this one here by Papunya Tula artist George Tjungurrayi, helps to give the piece a sense of place.

MATCH ART TO THE ROOM
↑ Choose art that is related to the room in which it will live. Jessie has chosen naive art by Margo McDaid for the walls of the children's playroom.

Art comes in many forms

Having pieces of art in your home doesn't mean spending lots of money on one-off original paintings. You can also frame the following:

- Gift cards
- Pages out of books
- Book covers
- Photographs
- Sketches
- Secondhand finds
- Dried flowers and foliage
- Collections like matchboxes, bottle tops, cinema tickets, travel memorabilia and so on
- Children's paintings
- Plates and other pieces of china
- Cushion covers
- Tea towels

THE WALL AS A FRAME

The beautiful works on this page match the strong wall colours behind them. It's almost as if the walls are providing an extra frame. The stunning artwork by Stephen Thorpe (left) echoes the colours in both the caramel wall and cushions and the green sofa.

Wall hangings

Wall hangings are a great way to create a WOW factor because they are primarily designed in a large format, they take up a lot of wall space, and you can't help but turn your head when you walk past.

Wall hangings are traditionally hung from a piece of dowel strung through loops at the top of the fabric. This hanging technique helps to keep the fabric perfectly straight, so it doesn't sag. The dowel for the striking wall hanging by Raby-Florence Fofana for Slowdown Studio (right) is resting on a pair of coat hooks on the wall. You could also achieve a similar effect by hanging a large kimono, blanket or patterned rug, for example.

Future-proofing

Thinking about how you and your family might change and evolve in the next few years is wise. Here are a few things you could think about doing to future-proof your own home.

- If replastering a wall, then ask an electrician to add wall sockets in places you might need them in the future.
- Establish where you could place a reverse cycle air conditioning unit on a wall in your home.
- If you are considering buying a bed for your kids, is it worth getting a double bed for them now rather than a single and then having to upgrade in a few years?
- Think about installing twin sinks in your bathroom instead of a single one.
- If you are replacing a ceiling light, is it worth putting in a light and ceiling fan combination? The world is getting warmer, and ceiling fans are a very popular option in the USA and Australia. They are becoming more commonplace in the UK too.

- Buying furniture that is multipurpose, such as a coffee table with added storage, a dining table that extends, a sofa bed instead of just a bed, and kitchen unit tops with extendable pull-out trays to increase your bench space.
- You might think about widening the gap between the kitchen island and the main kitchen units, so it's wide enough for a wheelchair. The same goes for widening the front door.
- Install bathroom grips in the shower for when you are older. We have them in our current rental home, and I find them useful – even in my thirties!
- Consider installing some underfloor heating (see page 88) if you are laying a new floor – it's lovely to feel the warmth underfoot.

- Get an electrician to fit wiring cables on either side of your bed, which is often necessary in older homes, so you can have wall lights wired in further down the line.
- Water-efficient additions to the bathroom and kitchen are a must – showerheads, loo flushes and so on – to limit water use.
- Plan for a future electric vehicle charging station.
- Replace single glazing with double glazing when you change your windows.
- Place furniture on castor wheels, so you can roll it out of the way when you throw a party.

THINK AHEAD
→ India has had sockets wired into the wall above the fireplace, but covers them up with a large poster for an Andy Warhol exhibition. Currently, India and her family don't watch television in this room, but they are likely to when the children are a bit older – so they have future-proofed the room.

1.

2.

3.

4.

Floors

The type of flooring to use is one of the biggest decisions (both creatively and financially) that you will make if you are replacing an existing floor in your home restyle. I suggest using the same flooring throughout each level of your home, so your interiors feel seamless. Many people opt for warm flooring like carpet in bedroom areas and a hard floor in the eating/living areas, so it's easy to clean up spills. Here are eight types of flooring that you could consider when doing your research.

1. Vinyl flooring

Made from layers of synthetic material, sandwiched together to make it durable.

Pros:

- Stain-resistant and waterproof
- Hard-wearing and can handle high-foot traffic areas
- Easy installation and low-maintenance
- Affordable

Cons:

- Hard to remove once glued down
- If you use a roll of vinyl and it is damaged, it can't be fixed – instead, use vinyl tiles and just remove and replace one or two

2. Engineered timber flooring

This has a natural hardwood top layer and cheaper wood on the bottom layer, which helps reduce the cost.

Pros:

- Natural product
- Looks like solid wood but is available at a cheaper price
- It comes pre-finished, so you don't have to seal it once laid
- Easy to repair since you can replace individual boards.
- Does not warp

Cons:

- More expensive than vinyl
- Can scratch and fade over time

3. Stone floor

Tiles made from natural stone from quarries.

Pros:

- Highly durable against high foot traffic
- Natural and eco-friendly material

Cons:

- Needs to be sealed because stone is naturally porous
- Since stone floors are made from a natural material, they are susceptible to chipping

4. Reclaimed flooring

Wood flooring that has been salvaged from an old building site or similar.

Pros:

- It is good for the environment to use any kind of secondhand materials
- Every floor is unique and comes with its own story
- The flooring might have an interesting colouring or patina

Cons:

- Durability depends on the wood and from where it was reclaimed
- Reclaimed flooring can be expensive due to all the labour involved in preparing and installing it. If the flooring is reclaimed from a salvage yard, it needs to be stripped and made ready for laying again, which is a long and fiddly process

5. Parquet wooden flooring

Pros:

- A timeless herringbone pattern that has been well loved since the 1500s
- Visually stunning
- Hardwood is a natural material

Cons:

- You will pay a lot more for a parquet floor due to the large number of pieces and the time it will take to install
- It will need care and protection over time to prevent scratches and other damage

6. Encaustic tiles

Decorative tiles in either cement or porcelain. (The ones shown here are cement.) I recommend you research encaustic tiles, as there are many conflicting reports about how to lay and seal them correctly. Cement encaustic tiles have the colour and design all the way through, so if they chip you will still see the pattern underneath. This generally means that they will age well – as they have in European homes for hundreds of years.

Pros:

- Encaustic tiles have had a resurgence in popularity over the last 10 years, so there is a wide choice available now, including many bold, bright and fun patterns
- Durable and will cope with heavy/ high foot traffic

Cons:

- Concrete tiles will wear and age as time goes by – although this might be a pro for some people
- The tiles can have a porous finish if they are not sealed correctly – plus it can be difficult to seal this type of flooring well too.

7. Brick

Traditionally made from dried clay, although chemicals are now added to modern-day bricks.

Pros:

- Beautiful, textured, matte finish
- Good for hiding dirt due to its rustic appearance
- Can withstand extreme conditions. Some brick floors are still in place after hundreds of years
- Virtually slip-proof

Cons:

- Bumpy underfoot (actually a pro for me, as I like the uneven tactile nature of brick), which can lead to falls
- Requires sealing to protect from stains

8. Polished stone

A type of floor that can be used seamlessly both inside and outside the home. Shown opposite is classic travertine, a form of limestone.

Pros:

- Natural material from a quarry

Cons:

- Surface needs to be sealed periodically
- Cold underfoot unless underfloor heating installed
- Expensive

Underfloor heating

This form of central heating is laid under the flooring to warm your home and your feet when it's turned on.

Pros:

- Can distribute heat more evenly through the home than a radiator
- Easy to run
- Increases the value of your home
- Is not a huge additional expense if you are laying a new floor anyway

Cons:

- Costly to install and retrofit if you're not already in the process of replacing your floor

5.

6.

7.

8.

Lighting

Lighting is a key part of any room scheme. To integrate lighting thoughtfully into a room, you first need to think about how the space will be used and what you want to achieve – for example, reading, entertaining or highlighting a piece of art on the wall. Think about lights as the jewels in your home, giving out just the right amount of sparkle when required.

PLAN YOUR LIGHTING

I suggest drawing a floor plan of the room and then drawing circles in the areas you will use for a specific task, such as reading or displaying art. This will help you understand where you need to light the room. If you turn on one light in a dark room, it will enable you to see areas in the space that will remain in shadow. However, you will need multiple light sources if you want every part of the room lit up to help you perform specific tasks.

On this page and opposite are four recommended light sources to illuminate your room successfully – you can mix and match these as you wish.

1.

Ambient lighting

This is powerful lighting that can light up an entire room (it is best placed symmetrically in a grid pattern). Try:
- Ceiling and wall-mounted fixtures
- Downlights (these are known as downlights because they shine the light from the ceiling)
- Track lighting

2.

Task lighting
This helps you perform specific tasks like reading or cooking.
- Desk/table lamps
- Under-cabinet lights
- Downlights
- Pendant lights (hung 70–80cm/28–32in above the tabletop)

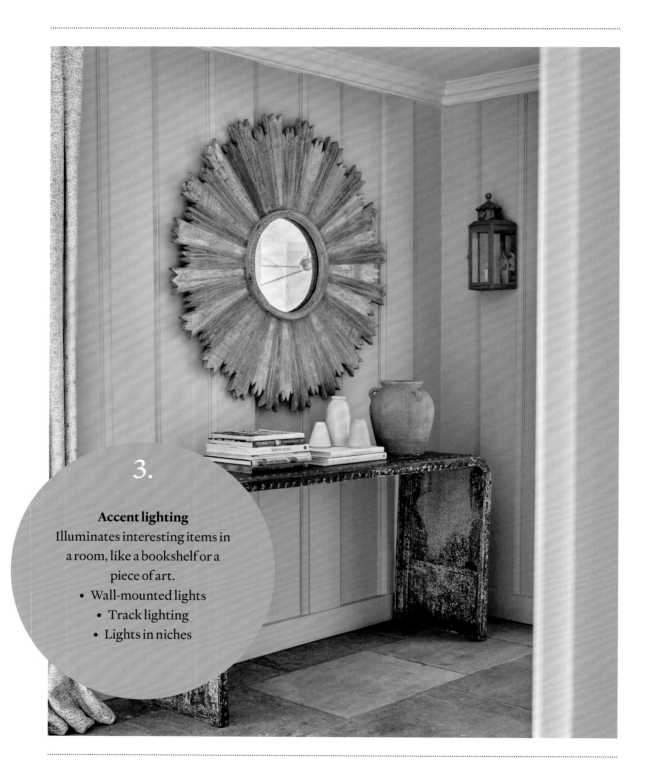

3.

Accent lighting
Illuminates interesting items in a room, like a bookshelf or a piece of art.
- Wall-mounted lights
- Track lighting
- Lights in niches

4.

Decorative lighting

This is statement lighting that shines an interesting light around the whole room.

- Chandeliers
- Floor lamps
- Fairy lights

What is an IP rating?

An IP rating – also known as an International Protection Rating – is an international standard that represents how waterproof a light fitting or device is. The scale goes from IP00, IP01, IP02 and so on, all the way up to IP69.

If you want to install a light in your bathroom (essentially a wet zone), you need to look for a light with the minimum IP rating for your country's electrical guidelines. All shops and manufacturers selling lights will know the IP ratings of their products, so look at the description and ask for professional advice before purchasing anything.

TOP TIP
Use one or more lights above a vanity basin to light up your face evenly when you use the mirror. Layer the lighting as you would for other rooms, with downlights and task lights working together.

LIGHT IT UP
↑ In the UK, light switches need to be mounted on the wall outside the bathroom. However, in many other countries, the light switches can be placed inside the bathroom.

CREATE A DESTINATION
→ Claire and Jamie's downstairs loo looks as if you have stepped into a tiny French café. The IP rating for these incredible pendant lights would be low, as there is little chance of water splashing onto the light fitting.

Storage

Storage is arguably one of the most important design factors in a modern home. You can maximize your usable space by including a mix of built-in storage, multipurpose furniture (like a storage coffee table or storage bench in the dining room) and functional shelving.

Fitted wardrobes

Wall-to-wall fitted wardrobes make a space feel as large as possible. Simple, flat-fronted doors (with finger holes instead of knobs) are perfect for a minimalist style and help draw the eye up to the ceiling, making a room feel taller. This idea is especially clever if you have a difficult space such as an alcove, uneven walls or awkward corners in lofts, as it hides all the strange angles behind doors, for example, and looks straight and seamless when viewed from the front.

Bespoke-fitted furniture can be expensive, but I know many people who have used IKEA carcasses and then had MDF doors built to fit the front, which can keep the costs down.

TOP TIP
Historically, people have built fitted cupboards so they start 30cm (1 foot) below the ceiling, but that ends up creating dust and is a dead zone. Build as high as you can, I say!

FILLING A TINY GAP

Whenever I see a spare sliver of space, I build cupboards. Extra storage makes a home feel curated and personalized. Here, Christabel has used tiny shelves to accommodate some of her favourite books – and because it's painted in her signature pastel shade (a thread throughout her home), it ties the rooms together. These small bespoke additions can be made from floorboards or timber left over from a renovation project.

LOG STORE
Building a log store in a living room rather than outside can have a double benefit: somewhere to keep logs and a shelf for the TV. Here, evenly cut firewood looks superb as part of Lotti and Andrew's palette of neutral colours and rust tones. The George Young painting in the alcove helps to lift the space with its pastel shades. What could have been dead space has been cleverly transformed into something that connects form and function.

A NOTE ABOUT NICHES…

Niches are the pockets of your home! Introducing a shallow alcove in a wall allows you to display your treasures or anything you need conveniently stored. Niches are perfect in a bath or shower area and a kitchen, and can also be an exciting design detail down a hallway – especially if lit up with a strip of lighting.

How to connect rooms

One common design dilemma is how to link two adjacent rooms and, indeed, the whole house. The key is to 'connect'. The two (or more) rooms need to feel connected by something, whether that is a colour or a pattern, or a story, theme or trend, with colour being the most common method.

To work out how to connect two rooms using colour or pattern, stand at the spot where you will naturally see both spaces simultaneously (in a doorway, for example) and think about your view as a vignette. Then stick to your mood board and a minimal palette to help you decide which colours and patterns to employ as your connecting feature.

Keep returning to what YOU love. If you love neutral tones and light, bright spaces, then stick with that thread.

CREATE A CONNECTION
← Caroline has continued her thread of calm, cool, muted pastel shades throughout her beautiful home. The wallpaper in the hallway has a two-tone leaf pattern in cream and green. The cream is the same as the wall paint, while the green ties in with the pastels around the house and the greenery in the country garden.

REPETITION OF A THEME
→ Repeating textures, colours, materials, themes and features from specific periods around the home, will help the space feel both cohesive and individual. Claire and Jamie's home is brimming with wonderful, eclectic pieces that all hang together because of the repeated use of the same materials and surfaces. Vintage wooden cabinets, tables, chairs and work surfaces are all part of the couple's signature reclaimed vibe. They have built a fantastic business out of preloved furniture and have continued that story throughout their own home.

Repetition of materials

You can pull everything together visually and connect it all by using the same material throughout your home. This material might, for example, be panelling or textured wall finishes, such as plaster or wallpaper, or the same flooring throughout the various rooms.

If you are undertaking a home renovation or restyle, it pays (from a visual and resale perspective) to have the same flooring all the way through. Many unrenovated houses have multiple types of flooring, with a joining strip along the floor at the threshold between each room, which creates incontinuity through the home.

If you would like a change in flooring, you could choose something different for each level of the home (for example, the ground floor could have floorboards and the bedroom level be laid with carpet). But pulling up the floors and laying a new seamless material throughout – whether this is timber, rubber, vinyl, carpet or polished concrete – will make a world of difference.

A VERTICAL CONNECTION
Dan and Nina have used a vertical pattern throughout many spaces in their home (and on the outside, too). The cinema room is painted dark blue, while the kitchen has been left with a natural finish, but the vertical line repetition using Siberian larch leads you through the house.

Continuity of colour

Anna and John's beautiful colour
palette continues through every
room of their home. Above is their
loft bedroom looking through to
the ensuite bathroom. You can
see how the mood board has been
continued from the dining room
(top right) to the top of the house.

TOP TIP
I suggest you break
up your mood board into
different sections and use
these in different rooms. It
is the same palette but in
different proportions
around the home.

LOOK CLOSELY

At first glance, you may not notice the continuity of the colour palette in these two rooms in Matt's home. But take a closer look and you will see the repetition of tongue-and-groove panelling and colours: soft grey-green, white, mid-tone wood and yellow ochre, with a touch of black.

	Kitchen	**Bedroom**
Grey-green →	Wall panelling	Blanket, art print
Yellow ochre →	Oil painting	Bedside table
White →	Sink	Bedding
Black →	Window	Art frame
Brass →	Taps	Luggage rack

How to style an open-plan space

My quick tips for styling open-plan living:
If you have an open-plan home, you will want to style the adjacent rooms as one cohesive space.

- The space will look much more desirable if you try to keep the furniture away from the walls and towards the centre of the room. Pushing everything up against the walls makes for a big empty space in the middle of the room.
- Try to style with pieces of furniture that don't have high backs – aim for lower furniture all the way here.
- Rugs will be your saviour, helping to zone a space subtly, but you will need large rugs, which can be pricey (buying secondhand can help with this). Selecting the largest rug you can afford for your room will always look best.
- Try to keep the flow of the room open. That usually means having the sofa opening out into the space, so you don't have your back facing another room.
- You must stick to your minimal colour palette in this scenario. Don't introduce too many colours into an open-plan format – it will look too busy.
- Have consistent flooring throughout the connected spaces.
- Use a freestanding room divider if you decide to place a piece of furniture in the middle of the room and want to create a vignette by having a backdrop behind it.

STICK TO THE RULES

Elisabeth and Aldo have stuck to the rules of styling in their open-plan house. The furniture is away from the walls, the sofa is facing into the room, the pendant light helps to zone the dining area, and they have also kept their colour palette consistent.

TOP TIP
If you love the look of
the original brick wall here
at Elisabeth and Aldo's house,
then you could do something
similar at home by using
brick slips to tile the wall or
by hanging a brick
wall mural.

Hidden design details

We all have spaces in our homes that are dead zones. For our houses to work smarter, we need to think about how a space might have a double function, so we can maximize its functionality.

HIDE YOUR TELLY

↗ Goodbye, black box! You can hide your TV, as Lotti has, by recessing a curtain track so the curtains are flush with the ceiling. The curtain track goes across the room (as opposed to having one short rail above each window, which is more common), so the TV can be hidden during the day behind floor-to-ceiling curtains.

IT'S A DOG'S LIFE

← Caroline's kitchen island works on many levels – for cooking, working, kids' homework and housing the family dogs in the built-in dog bed underneath. I love this idea, as it means you're not tripping over the bed somewhere in the middle of the room.

KEEP IT HIDDEN

→ You could hide away the TV when it is not being watched by using a sash window pulley system that allows the two doors to meet in the middle, as Dan has done here.

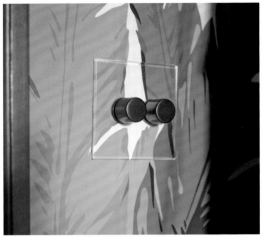

FANCY FITTINGS

↑ I love the clear acrylic wall plates that you can buy for light switches. It means that whatever wall covering you have can be seen through the plate. A subtle touch and genius design detail.

SMALL LUXURIES

↑ Try using brass door furniture as an easy update around your home. It's a treat to have glimpses of luxury used for something that would otherwise be dull. But beware, you can pay a lot for brassware if you install 20–30 door handles, knobs and knockers around your home – it all adds up! To keep the cost down, you could have them only on the doors you use most often or in a busier part of the home, such as the kitchen or living room.

Plants

Having plants in your home is good for your health and can be a fantastic styling tool to fill an empty space. The cost of large statement greenery (like monsteras, fiddle leaf figs and banana plants) can be prohibitive, so I suggest buying smaller baby plants and helping them grow – they're half the price that way.

CASCADES OF GREEN
→ Suspending plants from the ceiling on a rack, as Dan has done, provides something beautiful to look at, but it is also functional, as it gives the plants a stable platform to hang from.

PART TWO

THE ROOMS

KITCHEN

This chapter will provide a more in-depth look at some incredible kitchen spaces and how their owners have styled them. The kitchen is the heart of the modern home – it's where we cook, prepare food, eat, entertain, work and socialize. Our kitchens are having to work harder than ever, and the stunning examples over the following few pages will hopefully inspire your next makeover. Whether you love bright colours, muted tones, bright white or pastels, remember there is no 'right way' to style a room, so start with your mood board, find a style that you love, and stick with it throughout the project.

The character kitchen

HOME: ANNA AND JOHN ● TERRACED HOUSE, EARLY 1900s

Anna and John's vibrant kitchen couldn't be more characterful. It is a Shaker-style kitchen and combines burnt orange cabinets and a sage-green kitchen island. Both units have been finished with brass accents and topped with Carrara marble worktops, the brightness of which helps to bounce light around the room.

Note the hidden gem here: instead of a traditional tiled splashback, Anna and John painted the bottom third of the wall in a high-gloss, wipeable paint (in the same colour as the rest of the wall). You can hardly see it in the photo, as it is such a subtle design element, but it means the splashback can be wiped and is more resilient.

The mood board

When you gather together some of the favourite trinkets you have collected over the years, you can often see your bespoke colour palette coming to life. Let those objects guide you – they might be:

- A box of matches
- A white enamel soap dish
- A notebook
- A brass number
- Your favourite spoon
- A pencil

Sometimes, when you are asked what your style is, it can be hard to put it into words. But when you start gathering together the items that you already own, then you realize that you had your very own style all along – it just took this creative task to make you realize that you do.

SHOWCASE YOUR FAVOURITE THINGS

← Building a shelf around the kitchen cooker hood is a great way to provide an extra surface for showing off beautiful crockery and a treasure trove of art and collectables curated over the years.

ADDED STORAGE

→ You should always squeeze storage in wherever you can. Here, shallow shelves have been built into the side of the kitchen island to house all Anna and John's Kilner jars, which are full of spices and legumes. It makes for a pleasing and functional space that would otherwise go unused.

Inner city living

TOP TIP
If you run floorboards from left to right, the room will appear wider. Conversely, the room will appear longer if you lay them from the front to the back.

A TALL ORDER
→ The couple like to stack their white crockery in an ordered and accessible way. Rows and groups help to keep things under control. There's nothing too stuffy here – it's real life on show!

This beautifully streamlined kitchen is a masterclass in simplicity. For example, check out the handle-less kitchen cabinet doors – the tops of the doors are chamfered at an angle so you can pull them open easily without handles.

Open shelving gives you the chance to showcase your favourite things. This colour palette feels as if it has been lifted from a Scandinavian coastal scene: the pale blues, white, sandy tones and pale matchstick flooring are a winning combination. The blue of the cabinets looks like the sky, while the pale floorboards are like the sand – we can reference nature even if it is subconsciously.

The beauty of earthenware is timeless. Natural materials will always have a place in the home – you can't help but want to pick them up and touch them. The pottery displayed on the shelves makes me think of sandy pebbles you might find on a coastal walk and is the perfect pairing with the blues of the cabinets.

The glassware along the top of the shelves is a great way to draw the eye towards the ceiling (remember it's always important to LOOK UP!), but without feeling messy or cluttered. The glass vessels fade into the background, so all you're looking at is their outline.

Unusually the kitchen unit top is made from ceramic, and the product colour is Concrete; hence it looks like a buffed concrete surface, and it's smooth to the touch. The beautiful vintage dining table and chairs within this smooth contemporary kitchen create a timeless look.

Blue Verditer™ 104.   ®

Air Force Blue™ 260.

The following items on the mood board (shown opposite) represent elements in the final scheme. It's amazing how a spoon can end up inspiring a dining table a whole year later. This is one way to translate a mood board into real-life items:

Patinated 'Y' stencil = dark metal shelving unit
Wooden spoon = dining table
Hammered silver 435 sample = kitchen unit top
White paint sample = main walls
Wooden coaster (top left) = flooring
Abstract art postcard (underneath) = abstract art on the walls
Black graphite pencil = metal supporting columns
Blue paint swatches = blue cabinets

The dream vintage kitchen

HOME: CLAIRE AND JAMIE ● DETACHED VICTORIAN HOUSE, 1880

Claire and Jamie are fortunate to own the beautiful reclaimed interior showroom Louisa Grace Interiors in Banstead, Surrey in UK. You can see that a passion for reclaimed vintage and antique furniture drips from Claire's fingertips. Every item has been considered and thoughtfully planned and placed.

To design a stunningly successful vintage kitchen such as the one shown here, it pays to have sourced your dream kitchen cabinets before the build begins. That way, you can design the layout with the exact dimensions ahead of time.

Claire and Jamie had two possible options when planning the design of their vintage kitchen:

- To lose a room upstairs and allow that triple-height space to become a feature of the home. This is the option Claire and Jamie agreed on, as you can see from the image opposite.
- Or to install a standard-build kitchen with a lower ceiling to allow room for an extra bedroom above it upstairs.

Brilliantly, Claire and Jamie stuck with their initial idea and managed to convince the builder to lose that upstairs room. High ceilings are one of the most desirable features for prospective homebuyers, so if it's the resale value that you are worried about when creating a fully bespoke room, don't be. The WOW factor will always win.

TOP TIP
When designing a bold room like this, which has so many interesting design features, you can save money by buying simple splashback tiles that disappear into the background. Some things ought to be simple!

Surfaces

White, pale or light wood-coloured surfaces reflect the light, giving you a brighter room. Dark stone and wood will soak up the light and bounce less around.

Lighting

Low pendant lights over a sink help with tasks such as washing up. You should ideally hang pendants (like the ones above the sink opposite) so the base is at least 75–90cm (30–35in) above the sink or work surface. Other downlights can provide the necessary lighting for activities such as cooking and kids' homework. In this kitchen, the chandelier (fitted with light bulbs) helps with mood lighting when the sun goes down or if there's a party!

Bringing the outside in

Instinctively, we prefer heavier colours in the lower half of a room, which gradually become lighter towards the top, as this mimics nature (think of dark ground and a bright sky). You can see a perfect example here: darker wooden cabinets at the bottom and cream wall paint as you go higher.

Claire chose an L-shaped kitchen with a separate island, sourcing everything vintage to match her home aesthetic. The kitchen sink and the pendant lights have been placed centrally in front of the large window to give a feeling of symmetry, and all the furniture and accessories relate to the mood board.

A note about kitchen planning

The kitchen is arguably the heart of every modern home. It has to fulfil many functions. Not only is it where food is prepared and often eaten too, but it's also a space where friends and family are entertained, homework is completed, a range cooker heats the home, discussions are held and the dog sleeps...

Since a kitchen must work in so many ways, I usually recommend designing it in a fairly neutral or soft-coloured scheme. For example, a bright purple kitchen might work if you entertain and eat there, but if you want to work or study from a kitchen island, warm dark colours will be too overpowering when you're trying to stay focused.

The kitchen layout
Think about the layout of your kitchen before you plan anything else. There are various options for laying out a kitchen, which are presented here:

GALLEY KITCHEN
For long slim spaces

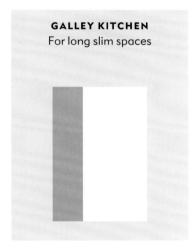

L-SHAPED KITCHEN

U-SHAPED KITCHEN

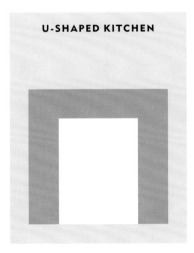

SEPARATE KITCHEN ISLAND
Plumbed or not

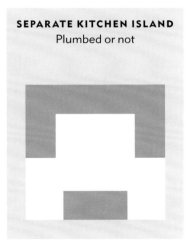

KITCHEN PENINSULA
An island where one end is attached to the wall

The eclectic home

HOME: JESSIE AND IVO ⊛ REGENCY HOUSE, CIRCA 1820s

Colour can absolutely transform a space. Take the deep lime-green shade shown here (Pale Lime from Little Greene), which Jessie chose for the kitchen island. What a colour!

You might look at this beautiful space and think you must be brave to choose such a bold shade, and perhaps you do. But think about where this colour palette exists in nature or design, and you'll realize that it can, in fact, work with the right ratio of colours.

Compare the image of Paris (below left) and the images of the kitchen. Paris has a small number of green trees and a large amount of neutral-coloured stone, concrete and sky. Jessie has used the same ratio of green to neutral in her kitchen. Remember, you can always look to the landscape for inspiration and use this to your advantage when styling a space.

The modern woodland kitchen

HOME: GUY AND KITTY ◉ GARDEN COTTAGE, BUILT 2021

Boards are not just for the floor – they are a surface texture, after all. So why not install them on the ceiling, walls and cabinets, as Guy and Kitty have done in their kitchen?

The idea of 'bringing the outside in' has never been more appropriate, with people having stayed indoors for so long in the last few years due to Covid-19. From a psychological perspective, there has been a shift to people wanting the colours of nature and, indeed, natural textures in their homes, so they feel connected to the outdoors. In this cottage kitchen Guy has cleverly used boards on all the surfaces EXCEPT for the floor.

Although Guy has chosen a dark wooden board with which to clad some of the walls, this is balanced out by the natural light coming in from the window on the left and the large, plastered wall. The clever use of a reflective marble worktop also helps bounce light around. The room doesn't feel dark, but it does feel cosy.

Remember, if you have a decent amount of natural light coming in through the windows of your kitchen, you can confidently opt for a dark interior – just use the light to your advantage by including shiny surfaces like glossy worktops, mirrors and satin paint finishes.

The all-wood look can be softened by the addition of flowers, such as the dahlias, anemones and chrysanthemums that complement the interior, so perhaps plant some suitable varieties in your garden. These pretty flowers are from the garden, and the divine jewel colours of the blooms also feature in the artworks just above.

PICTURE IT

← Install a narrow, floating picture shelf to showcase your favourite artworks and liven up a room. The work on the left is by Kindah Khalidy and that on the right by Lakwena.

Opposites

When you are looking to create something unexpected in your home, try to think of the opposite of the standard approach. Swap the traditional for the unexpected:

- If it belongs on the floor, can it also go on the ceiling?
- If it's traditionally light, can you make it dark? (Think about wall colours here.)
- If something has always been made square, can you choose a rectangle or circle instead?
- Could you swap wallpaper for tiles on your living room wall?
- Why always paint the window frames white when you can have them in a colour?

Where design meets nature

The indoors and outdoors of a property are often intertwined, but perhaps not quite as much as in Dan and Nina's stunning home, where nature, architecture and design intersect harmoniously.

The couple cleverly used the repetition of three main features in their kitchen. First, the vertical strips of Siberian larch have been used to form the kitchen cabinetry and the external cladding of the home. The pattern in the pendant shades and the beams on the ceiling also mimic the cladding.

Second, the striking plant rack above the kitchen island gives you a reason to look up and study the hanging foliage they have used to create such a striking feature. The plants have been repeated throughout the kitchen as well as the rest of their home.

Last, the black-edged glass cabinets on the wall above the kitchen units have been repeated in a set of three. Each one highlights collections of glass and crockery more beautifully than the last.

The timeless kitchen

HOME: CHRISTABEL AND JASPER ◉ OLD VICARAGE, 16TH CENTURY

The decorative scheme of this beautiful and traditional family home is held together by the tight colour palette of pink and green and the farmhouse theme. Note the large kitchen island with its chunky butcher's-block top (as used historically in farm kitchens).

The AGA is kept on all day to warm the home and above it are hand-painted tiles that Christabel designed herself. With these painted tiles, the brass fittings, earthenware vessels and vintage breadboards, there's a whole lot of soul in this kitchen!

TOP TIP
Put a kitchen island on castors, so you can roll it to one side for a party, to create more usable space and maybe a dance floor. Note: this easy-win idea won't work with plumbing and appliances in the unit.

UNEXPECTED COLOUR
← I applaud Christabel and Jasper's use of colour here, as most conservatory structures are white. The sage-green shade is a pale neutral tone and doesn't detract from the kitchen's beauty.

Kitchen islands

These are popular due to their functionality and for the additional work surface and storage they provide. They also allow you to talk to your family and guests while you are cooking.

Not all islands are created equal, however, and here are a few tips to help you find the right one for you and your family. Let's consider how you need to use your island:

- How tall are you? How many cooks are there in your household, and are you all the same height? Taller people will need a higher island to feel comfortable. A standard-height island is 90cm (35in) off the ground; 95cm (37in) is ideal for a taller person. If you are of different heights, think about who cooks most often and compromise.
- How much space do you have in your kitchen? A smaller space will mean you need a narrower island. The narrowest you could get away with is 60cm (24in). Usually, the widest islands are 120cm (47in).
- You must plan to have around 90cm (35in) between the island and the main kitchen units. This gives you enough room to walk around comfortably and past another person. If you are in a wheelchair, then 90cm (35in) will also be the minimum.
- If you want to have bar stools at your island, you will lose storage space – you need to decide what is more important to you.
- Choose the surface material for the island wisely. A chunky butcher's-block top like Christabel's will age well and last forever. If you choose marble (white Carrara marble has been popular for the last decade), note that it can chip if you drop a pan on it and stain if you spill red wine.

The warehouse kitchen

HOME: ELISABETH AND ALDO ◉ **CONVERTED FACTORY, 1890**

Elisabeth and Aldo's home is situated in an old dog biscuit factory in London and is the most incredible conversion I have seen. It has a simple, open-plan layout and is packed full of clever design features. Adding modern design elements to an industrial conversion helps make it feel less homogeneous and more like a family home.

Through good design, Elisabeth and Aldo, the owners of Encore Reclamation, have celebrated the heritage of the building by using as many reclaimed items as possible, while also allowing the space to function as a modern family home. Aldo saved the wooden flooring from a London ballroom before it was demolished and painstakingly fitted it in the house. The kitchen cabinet doors are utilitarian in design and made from MDF and lacquered with glue. There are finger grooves between the doors, so you can open them easily without the need for handles. The couple chose industrial lights hung from the ceiling, which can be swivelled to help light up specific places on the worktop – all of which were reclaimed.

There is a rich palette of warm golden woods, yellow, black and green in this kitchen, which continues throughout every room of the house.

A HINT OF COLOUR
→ Painting the outer edges of the shelves bright yellow makes for a happy pop of colour when you open the cupboard doors. With so many quirky design elements in the kitchen, the couple decided on simple white metro tiles for the back wall so as not to take away from the striking vintage textures used. Cleverly, the artwork by Wolfgang Tillmans ties in with the kitchen's colour palette.

Why the warehouse look?
Although you may love the open-plan look and the feeling of a large living area, bear in mind that warehouse conversions are often cavernous spaces that need to be cleverly broken up into zones to feel like a family home. The warehouse look is right for you:

- If you love original architectural features.
- You have a fondness for vintage and preloved items.
- You're not precious about things feeling 'perfect'. The warehouse look embraces old-world imperfections. Old, patinated, uneven, tactile and rough-around-the-edges sum up the qualities of this look.

The modern extension

Many of us choose to move to find the house of our dreams. And others, who are often more adventurous, decide to stay and renovate and extend. India is in the latter camp and has created this beautiful, Mediterranean-inspired kitchen extension in her London family home.

When you are planning an extension, start by deciding on the aesthetic you'd like it to have and then think about how you will blend that with your existing house. India and Tom have seamlessly connected their new extension with the original house through the clever use of a minimal colour palette, which is used in every room of their home.

The two hero design choices in this stunning extension are the brick floor laid in a herringbone pattern and the pink cabinetry, which is painted in Farrow & Ball Pink Ground. The soft tone of the cabinets is less 'pink' and more 'plaster', and feels as traditional as it does contemporary – a beautiful, timeless shade.

India decided to lay underfloor heating under the brickwork, so now the family can pad around without shoes and pretend they are holidaying in Spain. (I am the same as India in that respect and love nothing more than taking my shoes off and connecting my feet with the ground. I think it is the Australian in me.)

TOP TIP
If you want to lay flooring in a herringbone pattern, then you will have to make more cuts in the material. Therefore, you'll need to adjust your budget upwards and order between 15 and 20 per cent more tiles than you would if you were simply laying them straight.

A note about worktops

Lotti and Andrew chose 90-cm (35-in) standard height worktops for the main units in their kitchen (see opposite), but the kitchen island stands at about 95–100cm (37–39in) high to make it more comfortable for socializing. This is the perfect height for standing around with a cocktail in hand! The single floating shelf in a marble that matches the worktop allows them to show off their favourite items of crockery. It also means that dinner plates are close to hand when needed. When people think about how to style a contemporary kitchen, Carrara marble is one of the first materials that comes to mind. It's the most desirable look around. But what is the difference between authentic natural marble and the less expensive versions?

Type	Description	Natural or man-made?	Durability	Price	Notes
Carrara marble	A high-quality, natural white or grey stone with attractive grey veining.	Natural stone, direct from a quarry.	• May chip if you drop a heavy pan on it. • Can stain because it is porous. • Will need resealing annually.	££££	• Each piece of marble is one of a kind.
Granite	A natural stone that is quarried in large blocks.	Natural stone.	• A harder stone and more durable than marble. • Can withstand hot pots and pans. • Reseal annually.	£££	• Heat-resistant.
Quartz	Engineered stone made up of pieces of quartz (plus other types of stone, glass and ceramic) bound together with resin.	Man-made product that includes pieces of natural quartz.	• Highly durable due to it being man-made. • Less heat-resistant, so can burn if a hot pot or pan is placed on top.	£££	• The stone is man-made and there are hundreds of colours. • You could have a sink made of quartz integrated into the worktop.
Corian®	An engineered stone made from acrylic polymer mixed with minerals.	Man-made engineered stone.	• A softer surface than stone means it can scratch or dent more easily. • Can burn more easily from a hot pot or pan.	££	• Can be formed into any shape, and a sink and draining board can be integrated into the surface too.
IKEA marble-look worktop	Laminate worktop that looks like marble.	Man-made.	• Decent durability but not heat-resistant. Never place something hot on a seam or the worktop could lift.	£	• Made from fibreboard. • Easy to install yourself, if you wish. • Least expensive option if you want the look of marble in your kitchen.

HINT OF BRASS
The contemporary kitchen cupboards have finger grooves instead of traditional handles. To keep things interesting, there is a metallic strip behind each finger groove, so you can see a hint of gold from wherever you stand in the kitchen.

A note about kitchen sinks, worktops and taps

SINK:
Single-basin, under-mount, stainless-steel sink

WORKTOP:
Ceramic

TAP:
Monobloc (which means one hole in the worktop), twin-lever mixer tap

SINK:
Single-basin, under-mount, ceramic sink

WORKTOP:
Marble with drainage grooves

TAP:
Aged brass instant hot water tap (this one is a Quooker)

SINK:
Single-basin, under-mount, stainless-steel sink

WORKTOP:
Carrara marble

TAP:
Pull-out mixer tap in chrome

SINK:
Double ceramic Belfast sink

WORKTOP:
Quartz granite

TAP:
Swan- or gooseneck, single-lever, monobloc brass mixer tap

The search terms below will help you to source your own dream kitchen fixtures and fittings.

SINK:
Single, under-mount, ceramic Belfast sink with matching draining board

WORKTOP:
Reclaimed oak

TAP:
Gooseneck kitchen tap with levers and two-hole, bench-mounted mixer

SINK:
Single-basin, under-mount, stainless-steel sink

WORKTOP:
Marble

TAP:
Monobloc, square-shaped, instant hot/sparkling water (from Quooker)

SINK:
Single ceramic Belfast sink

WORKTOP:
Oak

TAP:
Traditional pillar taps

SINK:
Single-basin, composite-material sink with matching draining board

WORKTOP:
Reclaimed timber

TAP:
Wall- or deck-mounted (extra plumbing is required before wall is finished)

DINING SPACE

Your dining room should be a stylish space where you wish to spend time. It should be sufficiently comfortable and friendly that your family will want to have dinner there, enjoy conversation and wind down at the end of the day, but also feel energetic enough to transition to a dinner party atmosphere for weekends and holidays. Every dining room will have a table and chairs, which are your big ticket items to buy for this space, so make these your first consideration. However, many people don't have a separate dining room and instead have an open-plan kitchen/diner. Here, the aesthetic will be dictated by the kitchen style.

Style considerations for a dining space

Choosing a table

- Ultimately the dining table will be the hero in this room, so it needs to be your first design decision. What shape are you after? How often do you entertain? How many people would be eating all at once? Buy a square, rectangular, circular or oval table accordingly.
- The perfect dining table should be around 110cm (43in) wide to provide enough room for your glasses, plates, food, etc.
- I suggest buying the largest dining table that you can fit in the space, so you have 90cm (35in) around each side of the table to the wall, to accommodate chairs and the movement of people walking around the table comfortably.
- Consider a table with drop leaves or extra hidden panels, so you can extend it when you have a larger dinner party.
- Circular tables don't have hard corners, so they allow for a free-flowing room – especially helpful if it's a thoroughfare room.

Which chairs to buy?

- You will need about 22cm (9in) between guests around the table to ensure they can all sit down easily and comfortably.
- If the room is small, you could have benches on either side of the table to save space. The benches can then be stored under the dining table when not in use.
- Chairs without arms also provide more space.

Installing lighting

- You will always want a good light source over your dining table. Opt for a dimmer switch, so you can reduce the light towards the end of a dinner party. Ensure you have enough lighting to light the whole table – not just the centre.
- Ideally, pendant lights should be at least 70–80cm (28–32in) above your head at the table, so you don't bump into them and are also able to see the person sitting opposite you.

Using rugs

- If you decide to define your dining space with a large rug, then make sure this is 60cm (24in) larger than the table on all sides, to provide ample space for the dining chairs to sit on top of it.

STORED AWAY

← Caroline's stunning dining space utilizes benches on either side of the table with linen cushions for extra comfort. The benches can be stored under the table after use.

Zone your space

If you have an open-plan area or a room with more than one use, zoning the space is an important part of styling your home. There are several ways to zone a space that can give it a creative edge.

Zone using panelling

John and Anna have designed a highly coveted dining area. To make the most of their shared kitchen/dining space, they cleverly installed a tongue-and-groove wall panel and painted it a glossy, fire-engine red. Above the panelled wall, they have installed a matching red shelf supported by brackets to display their books and objects. This design feature (and conversation starter!) is a relatively simple thing to replicate in your own home and helps to zone a room clearly. A built-in bench (with a lift-up seat for extra storage) means you can position the table closer to the wall, providing you with more room in the kitchen zone.

When John and Anna built their kitchen extension, they included a large-format picture window that starts about 60cm (24in) up the wall and allows for a window seat. The window can be opened on warm, sunny days, so you can view the garden (and a beautiful willow tree) from the dining bench. The vertical lines of the window mimic the vertical lines in the tongue-and-groove wall panel and this brings both features together visually.

ZONE WITH A RUG

Buy a rug that is large enough so all the dining chairs can fit on it comfortably without getting caught on the edges. Jessie's natural rug is big enough to sit comfortably under all the chairs, but small enough that the beautiful flooring can also be seen around the edges of the room.

ZONE WITH BUILT-IN SEATING

This covetable dining space is off the side of the kitchen and continues the colour palette used throughout this beautiful, open-plan home.

The built-in benches provide more seating space than average dining chairs and can be warmed up with some fluffy sheepskin covers.

ZONE WITH LIGHTING

← These three ex-factory, enamel pendant lights claim the space in Claire's dining room. They are suspended above the table from a large piece of driftwood. The electrical cable has been threaded through the driftwood to allow each light to work.

MINIMAL IS THE KEY

↓ Use a minimal colour palette to ensure all the elements tie together. This room is a mix of brown, black and white and works beautifully with the artwork by Guillem Nadal. The large pendant light is almost the same size as the dining table – a striking effect.

ZONE WITH SHELVING

This open-plan dining room/ kitchen is lined with floor-to-ceiling bookshelves, which add height and depth to the space and mean all the records are accessible when you want to play some tunes. Having items like these on show is much better than hiding them in boxes in a basement.

"A house without books is like a room without windows."

Horace Mann

LIVING ROOM

No other room needs to work quite as hard as the living room. It's for relaxing, entertaining, working, exercising and napping, so the form and function of every piece of furniture needs to be considered. When you style a living room, you need to think of a layout that will encourage conversation, as this will be one of the most social spaces in your home – the aim is to create a social space but with intimate qualities. Think about where you want your guests and yourself to face when you are sitting around. Do you want to face each other to hold a conversation, do you want to face the fireplace, or perhaps you want to look out the window to the garden? Ideally, you will decide on a permanent place for the sofa, as this is the largest item, and then you can curate the space with two or more armchairs that can be moved around, depending on how you use the room.

← Why does Jessie and Ivo's beautiful living room work so well? Because it's considered, edited down to a simple colour palette, and it also has SOUL. You can tell the space is loved and cared for and that it has been carefully added to over the years. Slow decorating plays a big part in producing a room of quality.

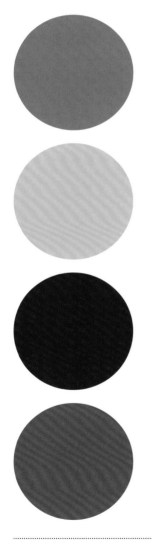

Functionality

As with every room of your house, you need to think about how you use the living room day to day. Carefully consider the room's functionality and, ultimately, how you want it to look. How do you use your living room? Here are some examples:

Helping the kids with homework	You will need a table large enough for at least two people to sit at comfortably with books or a laptop.
Relaxing in front of the TV	Incorporate a TV into the space. You could consider having a TV with a mirrored effect on the front, so it looks like a mirror when not in use.
Cocktails with friends at the weekend	Think about having a drinks trolley in the room to display your fancy bottles, or perhaps a shelving unit or cabinet to showcase your cocktail shakers and other drinks accessories.
Board games with the family	You could have a square fabric ottoman in front of your sofa with a large, flat surface, so you can play board games on top. That way, it doubles up when you want to lounge and put your feet up on it. If you have a wooden coffee table, you are less likely to put your feet up to relax. An ottoman gives you more options.
Yoga every morning	You could have your furniture on castors (the table, sofa, ottoman), so you can easily roll them to one side to make room for your yoga sessions.

Same colour palette three ways

I am often asked, 'I love these two colours, but where do I place them in the room?' My answer is that there is no right answer! If you love a colour palette, your choice of whether the colour goes into the furnishings or the walls won't matter too much. Take these three examples:

1.

2.

1. India and Tom's living room has a dark shade of green for the cabinetry, walls and fireplace and a caramel colour in the armchair.

2. Claire and Jamie's living room also has a green and golden brown combination. I love the shade of olive green they chose here.

3. In Anna and John's living room, the colours are reversed, with a gorgeous, green velvet sofa that sits beautifully in front of a caramel-coloured wall.

I suggest that if you have a perfectly good sofa in one of your favourite colours, then use that as your anchor for the room. Don't go and buy a new sofa 'just because'. Use it as your starting point instead.

3.

TOP TIP
When I am styling a room, I always work from the ground up, i.e. by choosing the surfaces first (walls, floors, windows), then the largest items of furniture, followed by the accents around the room.

ANCHOR YOUR SPACE
← Dan and Nina have chosen a tonal colour palette of soft pebbly shades and anchored the room with a deep teal velvet sofa. They have opted for a modest-sized rug as a large one would hide too much of that beautiful contemporary polished floor.

TEXTURED WALLS
← Dan and Nina's living room walls have been surfaced in Venetian plaster, which gives an organic depth to the surface that cannot be achieved with paint alone.

How big should a rug be?

There are two main reasons for using rugs in a room: to cover up a draughty floor and to keep the floor in good condition, preventing scuff marks. But with the rise of underfloor heating and a love for original aged floors, rugs don't always need to be as large as they once were.

Traditionally, a rug would have been large enough (approximately 3 × 4m/10 × 13ft) for the sofa, armchairs and coffee table to sit on it all at once. However, a rug that size is very costly to buy.

Contemporary advice is more likely to be that your rug should be large enough for at least the sofa's front legs to sit on, helping to keep feet warm and pull the zone together.

My advice is that you should buy the largest rug that you can afford. The bigger the rug, the more luxurious it will feel. Ideally, the rug will tuck under your sofa, so the legs are overhanging the rug by around 5cm (2in). But, like everything in life, you should do what feels right to you.

If you have a particularly beautiful floor (a herringbone pattern or a polished poured floor, for example), you only need a rug in the centre of the room to layer the space visually, so it doesn't cover up your design feature.

Decorating a living room with neutrals

A white palette in your home can make you feel calm, fresh and centred. A colour psychologist would tell you that white is associated with peace and harmony, and an estate agent would say that a white interior helps convey a positive feeling and a clean slate on which someone can write their own story.

The flip side is that white can feel clinical and 'un-designed'. However, the way to make a white room feel less dull is to explore the many tones and tactile surfaces available and style it with layers of texture. The homeowners of the rooms featured here have done just that. They have used height, light, layers and detail to make their rooms sumptuous and captivating.

Neutral textures you can shop for

- Metallics (silvers, golds, brass, copper, etc.).
- Wood (birch, oak, vintage wood, reclaimed floors, as well as limed and whitewashed).
- Fabrics such as linen, knitted, woven, lace, hand-knotted and velvet.
- Rugs and carpets, especially natural woven fibres like jute and seagrass.
- Paints in shades such as white, cream, putty, plaster, pastels, greys, pebble and stone.
- Some black accents can also help to pull the room together.

You can also include window shutters, tall skirting boards, found objects that tell a story, pale-coloured foliage, house plants, textured vases and vessels, pottery and earthenware. These will give the space added shape and dimension and ultimately create impact in the room.

Layers

By layers, I mean multiple textures on top of each other. For example, a herringbone-patterned floor, a jute rug and a shearling pouffe. These are neutral, with different textures, but tonally they are similar, and they create depth. This is your number one rule for making a flat room look more exciting.

Remember, one of the main reasons we care about interior styling in the first place is that we want the energy in the room to feel happy, warm, content and cosy, so people want to linger there.

TOP TIP
Removable slipcovers are a great way to keep a pale armchair or sofa looking clean.

POSITIONING THE ELEMENTS
→ Face chairs into the room to help promote conversation and give a sense of space. Styling your sofa by pulling it forward away from the wall helps to make the room feel bigger.

Furniture that fits your space

A well-styled home will always make the best use of the space that is available. We all know about built-in cupboards but often forget that you can order bespoke sofas too. A bespoke sofa can be costly, but you can also buy a modular one, which means you have more chance of getting the correct length.

GO MODULAR
← Matt has used the modular Söderhamn sofa from IKEA in his living room and put two of them together to fill the length of the wall. The room is topped off with a fancy green 'hat' in the form of a green-painted ceiling. (See pages 66–69 if you would like to learn more about painting ceilings.)

REPETITION OF A SHAPE
→ Guy and Kitty repeated the ellipse shape in their cottage living room with the ottoman, coffee table, armchair, sofa and pendant light, which all have a similar circular shape. Not only has the ellipse shape been repeated in the room, but the white panelling and gorgeous green accents have too.

STYLE YOUR DREAM CINEMA ROOM

Painting all the walls and the ceiling in this superb snug a deep colour helps minimize reflections on the TV screen. A wall-to-wall sofa means there is no wasted space and plenty of room for Dan and Nina's visitors. This type of room is achievable in your home by painting every surface in a dark hue – not black, but a rich dark shade that you love. Then either mount the TV or a projector screen on the wall.

BEDROOM

Your bedroom is one of the most personal rooms in the home. Therefore, this is the one room that you can decorate purely with yourself (and your partner) in mind. You don't need to worry about entertaining or how others will use it. Bedrooms are primarily for sleeping, so the decoration needs to be conducive to rest. Calm colours, soft textures, dimmable lighting and personal accents like art and objects are ideal. The most important items to source are your bed (I suggest buying the biggest one you can fit into the room easily – you will never regret it), bedside tables and lamps. Everything else in the room is a bonus. Then there is the TV. Whether to have one in the bedroom is a hotly debated topic (I am quite firmly in the 'yes' camp), but as it's your bedroom, no one else's opinion matters!

Styling the space with colour

Using colour not only adds warmth to a room but can also affect your emotions. You can use colour to make a room feel larger, an unloved space welcoming, and a chaotic room soothing. Pale, earthy colours, for example, are perfect in a bedroom if you wish to feel calm and grounded.

SOFT PASTELS

← John and Anna chose traditional panelling for their loft bedroom and painted it a beautiful slubby pink. Combined with the red bedside lamp and blue-green drawers, it gives a subtle Asian feel to the room. The large window bathes the room in natural light, which throws shadows along the panelling lines.

MATCHING PAINT TO TRIMS

→ One of my favourite bedrooms in the book is this fabulously quirky master bedroom in Jessie and Ivo's Regency home. The oversized faux doorway – like something that would lead you to Narnia – has been painted in the same colour as the exposed plaster walls, so it subtly fades into the background while still being visually interesting and a real conversation starter. Jessie used an approximate 60:40 mix of Jonquil and Rose from Edward Bulmer paints to achieve this colour.

COLOUR BLOCKING

You don't have to spend a fortune on a bedhead. You can take a leaf out of Elisabeth and Aldo's style book by fixing a copper pipe to the wall and hanging your favourite fabric behind the bed. The dark green fabric they chose helps retain the colour-blocked back wall as the room's main feature and they have styled the bed with various patterns and textures in the same colour group. Finding patterns that work together is easier if you stick to one colour.

Create a horizon line

Christabel painted the lower portion of the loft wall in Oval Room Blue from Farrow & Ball and continued it all around the room. The bed was then painted in Annie Sloan Chalk Paint® to match the wall. It's such a beautiful shade that it deserves to be the hero.

Lighting solutions

A room with no space for a bedside table means that there needs to be an alternate way to have lighting next to the bed. If you plan ahead, you can have an electrician wire in cables for wall lights on either side of the bed. If you want to have them wired in later, the electrician will need to chase the wall (cut it out), then lay the cables behind the wall and replaster it.

Alternatively, you could buy some simple lights with a very long flex that you plug into a wall socket. You can then drape the long flex around a hook in the wall and hang the lights beside the bed. No wiring is required here.

THINK ABOUT THE LIGHT

→ The blue paint is continued around Christabel's room, but on this side, the blue strip is much lower on the wall. This is because the window here is much smaller, so painting with more white helps to make the room feel brighter. The clever curtain under the bed hides the trundle mattress that provides more sleeping space for friends and family.

TOP TIP
Most of us have a piece of furniture that is the perfect size and shape, but we don't like the look of it anymore. Try painting it in a colour that is in harmony with the rest of your colour palette and see if that works! Use Annie Sloan Chalk Paint® – you can paint it on almost any surface, it doesn't need an undercoat, and it's perfect for decorative furniture painting.

Bed sizes

Most of us use our bedrooms only for sleeping in, so a large bedroom is redundant in most cases. A small bedroom can be styled perfectly to suit most people's needs. When styling, think about having the biggest bed that you can fit in the room without compromising on space for walking around it.

Don't forget that if you upgrade (or downgrade) the size of the bed, you will also have to change the mattress and all your existing bedding, so buying a new bed can be a costly exercise!

Average mattress sizes

UK	USA	Australia	Europe
Single 90 x 190cm (35 x 75in)	**Single/twin** 99 x 191cm (39 x 75in)	**Single** 92 x 187cm (36 x 74in)	**Small twin** 90 x 200cm (35 x 79in)
Small double 120 x 190cm (47 x 75in)	**Twin XL** 99 x 203cm (39 x 80in)	**King single** 106 x 203cm (42 x 80in)	**Single large** 100 x 200cm (39 x 79in)
			Small double 122 x 198cm (48 x 78in)
Double 135 x 190cm (53 x 75in)	**Double** 137 x 191cm (54 x 75in)	**Double** 137 x 187cm (54 x 74in)	**Double** 137 x 191cm (54 x 75in)
	Queen 152 x 203cm (60 x 80in)	**Queen** 153 x 203cm (60 x 80in)	
King 150 x 200cm (59 x 79in)	**King** 198 x 203cm (78 x 80in)	**King** 183 x 203cm (72 x 80in)	**King** 152 x 198cm (60 x 78in)
Super king 180 x 200cm (71 x 79in)	**Super king** 183 x 213cm (72 x 84in)	**Super king** 203 x 203cm (80 x 80in)	**Super king** 183 x 198cm (72 x 78in)

Preloved bedding

I like to buy good-quality, preloved, natural linen bedding. A lot of people initially find this very strange, but when I explain to them that when you stay in a hotel, you are sleeping in bedding that thousands of people have slept in already, it gets people thinking...As long as you wash preloved bedding well when you purchase it there is absolutely nothing wrong with it.

CREAM WALL, BOLD ACCENTS

→ If you want a calming, neutral and stylish bedroom, consider painting the walls in a cashew-nut tone. This is a warm, creamy white. There are only two colours in this room: blue and cashew cream. On repeat. And I love it. Neutral walls such as this mean you can change the accent colours more easily as the seasons change and your taste evolves. Warm, neutral tones are perfect for period homes. In contrast, greys are better used in modern, architectural homes.

TOP TIP
Don't forget the trusty valance, especially in neutral linen. Although less popular than in the past, they look great and can hide an ugly bed base. They are also perfect for concealing the space under a platform bed if it is being used for storage.

Symmetry

I am a big fan of symmetry, as it feels calm and harmonious and is visually beautiful. It also gives a more formal, grown-up look.

VINTAGE STORAGE
← Claire and Jamie have used two chests of drawers instead of traditional bedside tables in the alcoves beside the bed. Finding vintage furniture with the exact dimensions you need is no easy task, but Claire succeeded! Furniture that fits a specific space always feels more premium. Having a bespoke headboard made to fit the wall from end to end also makes the room feel more luxurious. To make this option more cost-effective, you could always buy some MDF, cut it to size, and upholster it yourself as a weekend project.

SEEING DOUBLE
→ Caroline has also opted for symmetry in the bright twin bedroom in the loft. Symmetry is a visually neat and tidy way of styling. This room's natural linen bedding and blue beach tones enhance the calm, relaxed, coastal vibe.

My quick tips for making your bedroom feel like a boutique hotel
Take a leaf out of Guy and Kitty's book and enjoy a plush hotel experience in your home every night of the week.

- Add a mattress topper to provide extra thickness and extra squish.
- Choose crisp, white bedding and include some extra blankets on top.
- Allow three pillows per person for more comfort.

- Make sure no wall is blank. This is key! Posh hotels never paint the walls – they are always papered.
- Stick to a maximum of two or three colours.
- A velvet bedhead, like the one below, is very luxurious.

BATHROOM

There are two types of people: those who love to take a bubble bath and those who don't. Baths may be practical for children, but taking a bath is often seen as a luxury for an adult. So the big question is: 'Do you really need a bath in your bathroom at all?' Once you have made that decision, then the other required items are quite standard, namely a toilet and sink. As always, your first step is to figure out how your bathroom needs to work for you and your family because there is quite a lot to fit into a bathroom. It is also usually a rather small room, so planning ahead is key!

Some ideas to get you started

Grab your notebook and jot down your thoughts on these points:

- Do you want a bath AND a shower? Many of us don't take a bath these days, opting instead for a wet room with an oversized showerhead.
- Do you want any shelving? Consider having a builder create niches in the wall instead of installing wall-mounted shelves.
- Double sinks are very popular nowadays. But do you really want – or even need – two?
- Depending on which sink and vanity unit you decide on, choose either wall-mounted or basin-mounted taps.
- Storage – at the very least, you will need somewhere to store the loo roll!
- You could always mount a basin on a piece of vintage furniture rather than buy a new vanity unit. A builder or plumber will then only need to cut a hole in the middle for the pipes to fit.
- If you have a bath/shower combination, would you prefer a shower curtain or a glass screen?

Stylish accessories for a bathroom

In terms of styling a bathroom with objects, the options are somewhat limited to what you find useful and can fit in the room without cluttering the space. To spruce up your bathroom, try:

- Towels that have an interesting texture, such as Hammam Turkish towels or those with a waffle weave.
- A stool for a book or magazine.
- Artwork (nothing too expensive here, as you need to avoid water and steam damage).
- Mirrors with an interesting trim.
- A floor mat or a wooden duckboard.
- Beautiful soap pumps (or a cake of soap on a soap dish – this is better for the environment as it doesn't come in plastic packaging).
- Wall hooks for hanging bathrobes and towels.
- Freestanding toilet roll holder.
- Indoor plants – these will thrive in a bathroom if there's a natural light source.
- A tray for trinkets on the vanity unit.
- A bath caddy to use when you're having a bath to hold your book and soap.
- Candles.

BATHROOMS CAN HAVE CURTAINS TOO
→ Lotti and Andrew's beautiful and sophisticated bathroom has a palette of white, plaster and marble, and a touch of gold in the lighting. Minimal colour choice is the key here. The floor-to-ceiling curtains in this room have a cocooning effect due to the beautiful, warm light that filters in.

Average sizes of bathroom furniture

If you are planning a bathroom makeover, it can be useful to make a floor plan to see what is possible in the size of room you have. This will also help you pinpoint where the various bathroom fixtures should go. Here are the average sizes of the main fixtures usually included in a bathroom for making a floor plan:

- Built-in bath: 700 × 1,650mm (28 × 65in)
- Freestanding bath: 1,520mm (60in) long × 760mm (30in) wide
- Toilet: 700–750mm (27½–29½in) high × 710mm (28in) deep × 500mm (20in) wide
- Bidet: 450mm (18in) high × 450mm (18in) wide × 500mm (20in) deep
- Single sink: 400 × 500mm (16 × 20in)
- Double sink vanity: 1,520–1,820mm (60–72in) wide
- A niche (or shelf) in a shower should be at chest height.
- A showerhead must be 200cm (80in) above the floor.

MICROCEMENT
→ Microcement is
a waterproof plaster
surface that creates a
smooth, seamless finish.
It can be tinted in any
colour and won't fade
over time. Microcement
is mould-resistant too,
which is a real bonus in a
bathroom. Here, I really
love the dusty pink paint
on the bedroom side of
the wall, which connects
beautifully with the grey
bathroom and helps
warm up the space.

IT'S ALL ABOUT
A CONNECTION
← Dan and Nina have
cleverly connected their
minimalist bathroom
with the bedroom on
the other side of the wall
by using the same wall
finish (Forcrete – a type
of microcement) and
colour palette.

STYLING YOUR BATHROOM

The multi-textured bathroom

HOME: GUY AND KITTY ● GARDEN COTTAGE, BUILT 2021

Interior designer Guy created this dream bathroom in his garden cottage using striped statement tiles as the hero feature in the room. Mounting panelling or striped tiles vertically or diagonally makes ceilings appear taller. These are encaustic tiles (see page 88), and their smooth, powdery finish is heaven to walk on. Guy stuck to the same colour palette in every room of their home.

TOP TIP
Substituting items on your mood board is important as you move through your house in order to give each room its own personality, while making sure you still stick to the original colours, shapes and patterns.

The room includes multiple patterns and lines, but because purple and green are complementary colours, they don't compete, but instead harmonize with each other. I like to call this the 'aubergine effect'.

This lovely space is just one of many bathrooms in the book with curtains. So, the next time someone says that you can't have fabric curtains in a bathroom, then tell them you absolutely can!

MY QUICK TILE TIPS:

- Try to overestimate how many tiles you will need and use tiles from the same batch. If you run out and need to buy some more tiles in a new batch, then the colour may differ.
- If you have any tiles left over at the end, you can resell them, use them as coasters, or tile the top of a coffee table or windowsill with them. If you have a full, unopened box, you can often get a refund from the stockist.
- Consider the grout colour that you will use when tiling. Use either a matching grout or a completely different colour (matching grout is more timeless).
- One way to tile on a budget is to buy inexpensive white square tiles (the most basic) and use grout in a fancy colour.

The pod bathroom

HOME: MATT AND NOEL

CONVERTED FROM AN 1853 SCHOOL IN 2014

It's like winning the lottery if you have extra space in the loft at home that you can extend into. The tricky part is how to design the room around the triangular shape of the eaves.

Matt and Noel opted to build a pod in their attic space, which is essentially a white box with a wet room and toilet inside – it's a genius idea. There's a clever clear acrylic box that acts as a conduit between the pod and the window above, so all the steam and heat can escape out of the roof. They placed the freestanding bath outside the pod, so the loft feels like a calm and zen boutique hotel.

SHOWER IN THE EAVES

A luxurious, cubicle-style shower is nestled into the pitched section of the roof line in Caroline's home. The use of glass doors helps to make the space feel larger, as any reflective surface will bounce light around a room and provide a feeling of space.

Slow decorating

Slow decorating means not decorating everything all at once. Most people find that moving into a new home sucks up their life savings, making renovating out of reach for a number of years.

However, there are a few things you can do to make a space your own while you are in the process of saving money to start your refurb. Art and mirrors, for example, are a simple, yet effective, way to stamp your personality on a room – as is the case with this large monochrome print by Sofia Lind (opposite) – especially if you plan to replaster the walls in the future because you don't need to worry about making marks.

FADED GRANDEUR
← This dainty sink curtain hides the bathroom gubbins behind it. Sink curtains are a timeless idea, so choose a timeless fabric, too – stripes and plain are an easy win. These look fabulous in a kitchen, bathroom or utility room. The beautiful patina on this old wall is very difficult to achieve if you are trying to create it by decorating. (In the industry, we refer to this as Faded Grandeur.) The only way to make a wall look like this deliberately is by buying a ready-designed wall mural. If you have a keen artistic eye, then you can also layer a few shades of Bauwerk limewash paint to create the effect. So, think long and hard before you plaster over a wall such as this because once it's done, you will never get it back to looking as good as Jessie's here!

VINTAGE + MODERN = TIMELESS
↓ Taking the time to find the perfect vintage piece is worth the wait. Here, the juxtaposition of a vintage mirror, ornate taps and a modern vanity basin is the perfect way to keep a bathroom looking balanced and contemporary. I always use old and new in every interior scheme to make it feel effortless. You can pick up any number of vintage mirrors at most charity shops, markets and antique stores.

The tone & texture bathroom

HOME: MATT AND KAT ● TERRACED HOUSE, MID-19TH CENTURY

Matt and Kat's gorgeous design palette combines golden tones, bamboo, warm weaves and classic panelling, and feels inspired by East Asia. The repetition of these tones and textures throughout their home helps to connect each room. In the bathroom, placing the bath under the arched window at the furthest end of the room provides a focal point in the space.

Painting a cast-iron bath

To add a splash of colour, you can paint a cast-iron bath, like the one shown here in reddy-orange. It can take some time (as you need a few layers of paint and a primer), but it could be a fun weekend job and will save paying the experts to do it. Here's how:

- First, prepare the painting area. Use dust sheets and take the feet off the bath if you can (otherwise just cover them with some masking tape).
- Mask off the top of the bath too, so you don't get paint on the enamelled part.
- Next, clean off all the dirt and dust.
- Apply a metal primer as an undercoat to stop rust forming and to provide a smooth painting surface.
- Wipe off all the dust again before the topcoat goes on.
- Modern eggshell is the best type of paint to use for the topcoat because you won't need to apply lacquer or varnish at the end.
- Use a paintbrush, roller or spray equipment to apply the topcoat.
- Apply two or three coats, making sure each layer is completely dry before starting the next.
- Apply a sealant at the end if you wish, but it's not necessary with modern eggshell paint.

Woven vinyl flooring

Matt's use of tactile surfaces is repeated in the main family bathroom. Woven vinyl flooring might seem an unusual material to use in a wet room, but here are some good reasons to use it:

- It feels great to walk on when you're barefoot.
- It can be used either indoors or outdoors.
- You can use it with underfloor heating.
- It looks like natural woven flooring (such as sisal or seagrass), but because it is vinyl, it has the added benefit of being waterproof.

One sink, two ways

Depending on your mood board and the vibe of your home, you can make the bathroom look completely different, no matter what your budget or design preferences. Here are two visuals to show how vastly different you could make one room using very similar items (the sink, mirror, wall lamp).

Blue bathroom

Caroline designed this calm, simple and stylish bathroom with dimensions similar to Anna and John's but opted for a muted statement wallpaper and contrasting scalloped mirror. Pale blue, white and a touch of black have a 1920s feel. Caroline has used premium wallpaper, but you can also opt for a less expensive option. Using a tall mixer tap like the one here gives a feeling of elegance in keeping with the rest of the room.

TOP TIP
Using a wall covering
will instantly make a
room feel more high-end.
Panelling or wallpaper
enhances walls in a way that
cannot be achieved with a
flat painted surface.

Orange bathroom

Anna and John built this amazing
bathroom when they renovated the
loft space of their beautiful home.
The couple's starting point was an
ornate cabinet (you can just see it
bottom right) and they decided to
build the rest of the room around
it. They echoed the timber with a
small wooden mirror and splashed
a burnt orange paint on the walls.
Adding a shelf to the windowsill and
behind the sink gave the room more
functionality – something that is easy
to do if you start a room from scratch.
A tall mixer tap would fight with the
shelf behind the sink, so these low
traditional taps work better.

Installing tongue-and-groove
panelling is more expensive than
wallpaper, but you could keep the
costs down if you have the carpentry
skills to do this yourself. Make sure
you think about the lighting early
on, as an electrician will have to wire
the exact spot behind the tongue
and groove for the light fixture.

Privacy

The bathroom is one room where privacy is usually a top priority, especially for those living in built-up areas overlooked by multiple homes.

HALF AND HALF

→ Café curtains are a brilliant way to make the most of the light coming through the top half of a window, while still giving you privacy in the lower half. The curtain shown here will work in any room of the house — and is especially helpful in countries where the natural light remains low for much of the year.

AN ELEGANT SPACE

← Dan and Nina have created a beautiful bathroom with soft light, shapes and shadows. To create privacy (and, indeed, a sense of drama), use full-length, soft voile curtains to keep your bathroom private and filter the light simultaneously. Hang them from a track in the ceiling to keep the look modern. If a bathroom was a ballet, this would be *Swan Lake*.

STYLING YOUR
HOME OFFICE

Many more of us are working from home now than ever before, but who would have thought a few years ago that so many employers would give us the flexibility to do this? However, it means we need a space at home to work from, which can be quite a luxury – not everyone has room for a dedicated workstation. You're lucky if you have enough space for a desk and chair, as many have to restyle their homes to allow for these. But regard this as an exciting opportunity to flex your styling muscles. Since you will most likely have to be at your desk for hours, your work area must be an inspiring space. The colour should make you feel happy and stimulated but not fretful and wired. Only you know which colour this is. Many people lean towards soft greens for an office, as it is both grounding and uplifting. With this in mind, perhaps consider soft green as your starting point if you can't think where to begin.

Homeworking

Here are some practical things you should think about when you're working from home:

- Do you use a laptop with a monitor? If so, you will need a surface area with more depth than usual.
- If you have regular video calls with work colleagues and clients, consider the backdrop that you would like people to see.
- Ideally, you will have the window on your left or right to get a nice sidelight for your video calls. Light in front of you will affect your vision, and light behind you will be too bright for the camera and cause glare on the computer screen. If your office desk has to face the sunlight, cover the windows with a sheer fabric curtain to dull the glare but help the room remain light.
- Are you tall and have long legs? If so, you will need a larger/taller desk. Consider an IKEA desk with legs that you can raise up and down (by spinning a disc at the base of the legs).

- Do you have an awkward space? Build a bespoke desk to fit.
- Do you have multiple types of tech that you use? You will need at least eight sockets in an extension lead to plug everything in. When you have plugged in your computer, monitor, printer, radio, Wi-Fi extender box, phone charger and desk lamp, it all adds up!
- Think about what you want to see above you on the wall. This should either be something calm to inspire you or something energizing to gives you the motivation you need to work.
- Use a chair designed for office work, as they are constructed with good posture in mind. If you sit on a dining chair all day, you will have a sore back. A good office chair is a more important purchase than the table you sit at. A table is just a surface, but a chair needs to support your spine.

DOUBLE USE

→ Guy has built a stunning wall-to-wall desk with cupboards at either end for the office space in his cottage. The office shares the room with the dining table, so the desk could easily double up as a bar when there is a party or more serving space is required. Towards the back of the dark green desk surface, you can see that an air-conditioning vent has been built in, which is helpful now that the climate is getting warmer. Sockets for phone chargers, a radio, and so on are easily accessible, but they can be hidden behind a photo frame, lamp or plant, for example.

GREEN SHOULD ALWAYS BE SEEN

→ Elisabeth and Aldo have used a calming green on the office wall here. It ties in beautifully with the curtains and vintage chair and is repeated throughout their home. The vintage desk is quite shallow and wouldn't accommodate a computer monitor, but it is perfect for a laptop. The large arched window is an ideal light source during the day, while the floor lamp next to the desk helps when the sun goes down.

THE ROOMS

Utilizing small spaces

Not everyone has the luxury of a dedicated office. Desks can be placed in alcoves and spaces with a small footprint. Let's not forget the kitchen/dining table – it will always be the default substitute office, no matter how hard you fight it!

To create a functional home office, you only require a flat surface for a desk, a chair and a computer, so you don't need more than 1.5–1.8m (5–6ft) of space. Remember, a successful space is all about the colour palette you choose.

TUCK IT AWAY
Guy and Kitty have built an office inside a cupboard in their kitchen. It can be closed away completely to hide everything when they have finished working. The doors fold flat to the side, so they are not in the way when people are walking past. There is even a box on wheels on the floor containing the printer. The office also acts as a central hub for the family to pin notes to the wall and file things away that they need easy access to.

CONNECTING SPACES

The secondary spaces in your home – for example, the hallway, staircase and entranceway – take you on a journey towards other rooms. I think you can make these spaces feel just as beautiful in your home, so I always style each space (no matter how utilitarian) with as much thought as my living room. Art, objects and collectables can be used to decorate a laundry room, entrance or hallway as you would in your living areas, and storage is the key. If you have ample storage in these connecting spaces, such as benches, cupboards and shelves, everything will have a place and feel much more curated.

First impressions count

Think of the entranceway as the room that paves the way to the rest of your home. What people see inside the front door is what they will assume the rest of the home is like throughout – so make that first impression count!

How do you use the entranceway?

- Do you have children and need a space for schoolbags?
- Do you walk your dog and need to wipe it down before you let it come inside?
- Are you a gardener and want to wash your hands as soon as you walk in?
- Do you need a completely clutter-free space, so you feel calm when you walk through the front door?
- Do you need a table lamp on a timer, so it turns on before you get home?
- Do you want the entrance to appear a certain way because you bring clients into your home?
- How much storage do you require?

HIGHLY STYLIZED

← Kitty and Guy have styled their entranceway in a harmonious palette of pink and green – it feels like a scene from a highly stylized Wes Andersen film. The tongue-and-groove vertical lines of the walls draw your eye up to the ceiling, making the room seem taller, while the tiled floor lines guide you to the next room and draw your eyes ahead of you. A cupboard storage wall clad in the same tongue-and-groove as the adjacent wall helps conceal items from view. The washing machine and tumble dryer are hidden behind these doors!

LIGHT AND BRIGHT

↑ Walking into a bright home can immediately make you feel more positive. India's entrance hall is calm and clutter-free, with a mirror to bounce light around. It all ties in with the colour palette established throughout the home – India used these floor tiles on her bathroom splashback too (see page 31).

A side entrance

An entrance hall doesn't have to be at the front of your home, it could be at the side or the rear. Either way, storage allows the room to feel organized, which is one of the easiest ways to help it feel decluttered and curated. Built-in cupboards to house the washing machine, tumble dryer, schoolbags, muddy shoes and so on will ensure the room looks and feels well designed. Don't forget to look at IKEA's PAX system to use as the carcass of the storage and build bespoke doors on top for the final finish. With the PAX system, you can configure any size and dimensions that you require; many professional interior designers use it too.

BUILD IT IN

→ This envy-inducing space is a purpose-built side entrance/laundry room where you can take off your shoes, wash your hands, store your bags and walk into the house dirt-free and unencumbered. You too can achieve this if you think mindfully about using a space that ties the room to the rest of the house. Although this room is a new addition to Claire and Jamie's home, it feels as if it has been there forever due to the use of traditional Shaker doors and large-format floor pavers. Claire has thought of everything. I love the single oak curtain pole in the recess for hanging delicate items while they dry. The washing machine and tumble dryer are in the cupboard to the left, hence the clever breathing holes on the sides to stop it getting too warm when the machines are running —not to mention the useful storage bench opposite the recessed sink where you can sit down to take off your shoes.

STYLE EACH ROOM AS IF IT'S SPECIAL

← Don't reserve your lovely treasures only for your kitchen, bedroom or living room. A utility room or bathroom can feel just as cosy if you add stylish elements such as pieces of art, vintage knick-knacks, plants and candles.

Styles and colourways to connect

Hallways and staircases are the connecting channels of our homes and they should be considered seriously when you are styling your space rather than being left as an afterthought. My advice here is to stick to your mood boards and colour palette for a seamless transition to the next level of your home. Let's look at a few different schemes – dark, light and neutral – and think about what is right for you and your space.

HARNESS THE LIGHT
↓ Black and white are timeless, chic and will never go out of style. Matt and Noel's staircase can be seen from almost every room in their open-plan house, so they have kept the palette light, bright and fresh to tie in with the home's aesthetic.

Dark

Matt has gone for a dark-on-dark scheme for his staircase, which is worthy of a private member's bar. The dark staircase and landing lead you up to the next level, where the bedrooms are lighter but still complement this paint colour.

Matt is very lucky to have a massive window where the staircase turns, as well as in the kitchen (behind the camera). This helps brighten up the whole space and throws light around. The dark palette wouldn't work if there were no natural light. Gloss paint on the staircase also reflects light back into the space.

Many modern staircases are built from concrete and are mostly covered in plaster, timber and/or carpet. However, you can leave the staircase bare if you want to showcase its raw beauty, as Lotti has done to good effect here.

A vintage vibe

Claire's eclectic home follows the same mood board palette through her hallway and staircase, but this time omits the darker colours and instead opts for lighter shades to help make the transition to the upstairs level, which is painted in mostly neutral shades (see page 34 for the full mood board). A popular effect on old staircases is to strip them back, leave the centre as raw timber, and paint the sides white. It helps guide the eyes up the stairs and here ties in well with Claire's vintage vibe.

TOP TIP
If you want a slim cabinet for the hallway, look at IKEA's top cabinets (made for a kitchen). They are shallow, so you don't bang your head when cooking. Add legs to the bottom and you have a hall table. Top cabinets are sold by all kitchen companies – for fancy doors and panels, take a look at Superfront.

BREATHING SPACE
→ Choosing a plain, large-format floor tile means that Claire's vintage finds have space to breathe. There always needs to be at least one pared-back surface in a layered scheme like this.

Flooring

To carpet or not to carpet your stairs? Points to consider:

- Are the stairs draughty? If so, a carpet can help to stop that.
- Do you have small children? Falling down the stairs is softened with carpet!
- Do you have the money for carpet? Carpeting can be pricey. It's less expensive to paint wooden stairs and leave them exposed.
- If you choose a patterned carpet for stairs that turn a corner, you will need to pay more to match the pattern on the corner seam. For this reason, it's easier to use a plain carpet instead.
- If you opt for a runner instead of carpet on the stairs, you can play with colour and pattern by contrasting it with the wooden stairs underneath.

If you create the WOW factor inside the front door, people will know what to expect from the rest of your home, and, as the image on the opposite page shows, India has nailed her contemporary look from the time you walk in.

TOP TIP
Using wipeable paint for wooden panelling is a sensible idea, as people can't help but touch a wall as they walk up and down a staircase.

ADDED CHARACTER
↑ Caroline's stunning neutral staircase is a triumph of simplicity, character and elegance. The wallpaper continues up the staircase to the level above and because it's so beautiful, it eliminates the need to hang artwork in the stairwell. Floorings like sisal, jute and seagrass are hard-wearing, warm and feel nice underfoot. If you choose a runner like this, paint the stairs underneath and the banister in a modern eggshell paint for the most hard-wearing effect. Do note, however, that natural flooring can stain easily.

DE-CLUTTER
→ Your floor space and staircase will look bigger if you keep clutter and decoration to a minimum. (Search for a 'stair basket' online – you can thank me later!)

A styling summary

Styling your home should be a mindful journey of discovery about yourself and your relationship with the space in which you live.

Your own story is unique, and the story of your home should be too. As you walk through the various rooms, you want to be surrounded by treasures that help you reconnect with past moments, so try to display things that matter to you and your family – don't hide them in boxes because you are unsure how to style them properly. Pull them out, place them on shelves, tables and trays, and start playing with new and different ways to display the objects you love.

Your home should make YOU happy, not anyone else. Styling your home can be as simple as filling a vase with beautiful blooms or as extensive as knocking down a wall in order to create a bigger space. If you want pink walls, do it! If you want a yellow kitchen, do it! Don't follow design trends; follow whatever it is that makes you tick. (Just stick to your minimal colour palette – you can do it!)

Remember these styling steps
- Think about how you want to use your space.
- Create a mood board.
- Collect inspiring images of other homes that you love.
- Decide on your minimal colour palette – remember that this should include textures as well as colours.
- Sketch some ideas.
- Decorate slowly and buy meaningful, long-lasting items.
- Begin to curate your space physically and implement your ideas one by one. Remember, this is not a race.
- Look back and enjoy what you have created!

Curate new spaces, create new stories, make new memories and collect new treasures that you will one day pass down to others. And, above all, have fun doing it.

I hope you enjoy your home-styling journey – wherever it may lead you.

Homeowners

A huge thank-you to the following homeowners:

Daniel and Nina Rowland
Interior Design and Architecture: @_studiofuse
studiofuse.co.uk

India and Tom Hares
Location house and home renovation journey: @ourhouseedit

Jessie Cutts and Ivo Vos
Artist: @cuttsandsons
cuttsandsons.com
Home renovation journey:
@townley_terrace

Christabel and Jasper Boersma
Location house:
@theoldvic_location

Matt Jowett and Noel Cottle
Location house:
lordshippark.com
(search for Canterbury Crescent).

Matt Peen
Pizza restaurant:
@hotwoodpizza

Guy and Kitty Wengraf
Interior Design:
@vitruviusandco
vitruviusandco.com
Cottage rental:
@our.country.place
ourcountryplace.co.uk
airbnb.com (search here for the garden cottage Little Tew)

Claire and Jamie McFadyen
Vintage furniture:
@louisagraceinteriors
louisagrace.co.uk

Lotti Benardout and Andrew Bredon
Location house:
@greenwoodroad

Elisabeth and Aldo Ciarrocchi
Reclamation company:
@encorereclamation
encorereclamation.co.uk
Location house:
@sprattsfactory
sprattsfactory.com

Caroline and William Pitman
Location house:
lightlocations.com
(search for a property called Cotswold Barn)

Anna and John Ferguson

Thank you to the location agencies that helped put me in touch with the fabulous people listed here:

The Location Guys
@thelocationguys
thelocationguys.co.uk
India and Tom's home
(Balham House)

Light Locations
@light_locations
lightlocations.com
Lotti and Andrew's home (London Fields)
Caroline's home (Cotswolds Barn)

PeaGreen Locations
@peagreenlocations
peagreenlocations.com
Jessie and Ivo's home (Townley Terrace)
Christabel and Jasper's home (Bridgewater)

Lordship Park
@lordshippark
lordshippark.com
Noel and Matt's home (Canterbury Crescent)

Resources

Here is a selection of my favourite places to shop that you might enjoy too:

Vintage/Secondhand/ Preloved
Lassco
lassco.co.uk
Louisa Grace
louisagrace.co.uk
Salvoweb
Salvoweb.com
The Old Cinema
theoldcinema.co.uk
UK Antique market directory
antique-atlas.com
Vinteriors
vinterior.co
Facebook Marketplace
facebook.com/ marketplace

Kitchens
Edward Collinson
edwardcollinson.co.uk
Pluck London
pluck.co.uk
Superfront
superfront.com

Upcycling furniture
Annie Sloan®
anniesloan.com
FrogTape®
frogtape.com
Harris brushes
harrisbrushes.com

Paint
COAT
coatpaints.com
Dulux
dulux.com
Farrow & Ball
farrow-ball.com
LICK
lick.com
Little Greene
littlegreene.eu
Mylands
mylands.com
Paint and Paper Library
paintandpaperlibrary. com
Porter's Original Paints
shop.porterspaints.com (Australia)
YesColours®
yescolours.com

Christmas
Balsam Hill®
balsam hill.co.uk
Cox and Cox
coxandcox.co.uk
Lights 4 Fun
lights4fun.co.uk
Liberty
libertylondon.com
Titania's Garden
titaniasgarden.co.uk

Rugs
Benuta
benuta.co.uk
Floor Story
floorstory.co.uk
John Lewis
johnlewis.com
La Redoute
la redoute.co.uk
Larusi
larusi.com
Urban Outfitters
urbanoutfitters.com
Woven
woven.co.uk

Fabric/Wallpaper/ Murals
Abigail Edwards
abigailedwards.com
Anaglypta
anaglypta.co.uk
Jessica Osborne
jessicaosborne.com
Mind the Gap
mindtheg.com
Poodle & Blonde
poodleandblonde.com
Romo
romo.com
Wallpaper Direct
wallpaperdirect.com
World of Wallpaper
worldofwallpaper.com

Door handles and hardware
Anthropologie
anthropologie.eu
Chloe Alberry
chloealberry.com
Etsy
etsy.com
Swarf Hardware
swarfhardware.co.uk
Zara Home
zarahome.com

Furniture and accessories
ARKET
arket.com
Fox Flowers
wearefox.co.uk
H&M Home
www2.hm.com
Heal's
heals.com
IKEA®
ikea.com
Nkuku
nkuku.com
OKA
oka.com
Rockett St George
rockettstgeorge.co.uk
Soho Home
sohohome.com
The Shop Floor Project
theshopfloorproject.com

Index

Accent colours 32–3, 177
air conditioning 84
architecture, influence 15, 17
artwork 55, 78–83, 131, 182, 191

Bathrooms 180–97
 accessories 182
 baths 11, 31, 182, 184, 188, 192
 curtains 182–3, 186, 191, 197
 furniture 182, 184
 future-proofing 84
 lighting 94
 in loft space 188–9, 195
 niches 99, 182, 184
 showers 182, 184, 189
 sinks/taps 191, 194
 striped tiles 186–7
 tone and texture 192–3
bedrooms 170–9
 bed linen 74, 176, 177, 179
 bedheads 59, 174, 178, 179
 beds 171, 175, 176, 179
 future-proofing 84
 storage 96, 175, 177
 styling 171, 172–5, 178–9
Benardout, Lotti & Andrew
 Bredon 98, 108, 140, 182, 212, 218
Boersma, Christabel & Jasper 50, 61, 97, 135, 175, 218
bookcases 40–1, 44, 152–3
Bredon, Andrew see Benardout, Lotti
brick 66, 88, 139

Castors, fitting 84, 135, 159
ceilings
 lighting 84, 90
 materials 131
 paint 66, 67, 68, 69, 166

chalk paint 61, 66, 74, 175
Ciarrocchi, Elisabeth & Aldo 106, 107, 136, 174, 202, 218
cinema room 103, 169
clutter 19, 207, 208, 214
colour palette
 bedrooms 171, 172–5
 calm colours 60
 choosing opposites 131
 connecting space 19, 30, 35, 56, 100, 104, 139, 211
 dark colours 34–5, 67, 72, 169, 210–11
 impact 55, 58–65, 67–75
 inspiration 14, 16, 128
 light colours 72
 living rooms 159–61, 164–7
 matching patterns 64
 minimal 28–35, 46, 58, 73, 159–61, 217
 neutrals 74–5, 164–7, 177
 open-plan spaces 106
 optical illusions 69, 72
 PREP formula 19
 styling basics 42
 tonal 46
 using single colour 58–9
 white schemes 73–4, 164, 211
concrete/cement 185, 212
conservatory, painting 63
Cottle, Noel see Jowett, Matt
cupboards 96–7, 203, 208, 213
curtains 108, 182–3, 186, 191, 197
cushions 56, 74, 147
Cutts, Jessie & Ivo Vos 42, 47, 60, 68, 70, 80–1, 128, 150, 152, 159, 172, 191, 218

Dead spaces 108, 203
dining areas 144–55

dog bed 108
doors 76, 84, 96, 110, 116, 219

Eggshell paint 66, 72, 192, 214
electrical sockets 84, 200
emulsion paint 66
entranceways 205, 206–9, 214
environment 77, 84, 87, 136
extensions, kitchen 138–9

Fans, ceiling 84
Ferguson, Anna & John 14, 62, 104, 116, 118, 148, 161, 172, 194, 195
fireplaces 61, 98
floors/flooring 86–9
 brick 88, 139
 connecting rooms 102
 heated 84, 88, 139
 materials 131, 136, 164
 open-plan spaces 106, 136
 optical illusion 120
 staircases 213, 214–15
 tiles 87, 88, 139, 207, 213
 woven vinyl 192–3
furniture
 bathroom 182, 184
 brass handles 110, 116
 creating impact 55, 56, 62
 entranceways 208
 fitting castors 84, 135, 159
 home office 200, 202
 living areas 159, 164–7
 multi-purpose 84, 96, 159
 open-plan spaces 106
 paint 66, 74, 175
 second hand 74, 77, 178, 219
 upholstery 53, 77
future-proofing 84

Gloss paint 66

Hallways 99, 205–15
Hares, India & Tom 30, 40, 44, 84, 139, 161, 207, 214, 218
heating, underfloor 84, 139
home office 198–203

Inspiration 15–17, 22, 34–5, 128, 217
IP rating 94

Jowett, Matt & Noel Cottle 49, 120, 188, 211, 218

Kitchens 114–43, 219
 eclectic 128–9
 future-proofing 84
 indoor/outdoor link 132–3
 islands 11, 135, 140
 lighting 125–6
 minimalist inner-city 120–3
 modern extension 138–9
 niches 99
 open-plan warehouse 136–7
 Shaker-style character 116–19
 sinks/taps 142–3
 splashbacks 116, 125
 storage 118, 120, 131–2, 140
 traditional 134–5
 vintage 124–6
 woodland cottage 130–1
 worktops 140–3

Laundry room 208
light 40, 131, 200, 202
lighting 90–5
 bedrooms 175
 clear switch plates 110
 dimmers 11, 147, 171
 dining areas 147, 153
 future-proofing 84

kitchen 125–6
on timer 207
living rooms 156–69
colour palette 159–61,
164–7
functionality 157, 159
furniture 164–7
loft spaces 14, 172, 175,
177–8, 188–9, 195
log store 98

Masonry paint 66
McFadyen, Claire & Jamie
35, 53, 94, 100, 125–6,
153, 161, 178, 208, 213,
218
mirrors 55, 94, 131, 159,
182, 191, 207
mood board 20–7, 104,
116, 123, 186, 217

Niches 99, 182, 184

Office space 198–203
open-plan spaces 106–7,
136–7, 152–3
optical illusions 69, 72, 120,
164, 186
ornaments 37–49, 56

Paint 66, 192, 219
panelling
bathrooms 186, 192, 195
bedrooms 69, 172
dining areas 148
entrances/hallways 207,
214
kitchens 102, 105
living areas 166
parquet flooring 88
pattern 64–5, 102, 186–7,
214
Peen, Matthew & Kat 58,
67, 83, 105, 166, 192,
210, 218
photographs 8, 14–15, 50
picture rails 81
Pitman, Caroline & William
64, 100, 108, 147, 178,
189, 194, 214, 218
planning 8, 19, 22, 90

plants 111
creating impact 55, 56
dried 52
in kitchen 131, 132
styling basics 40, 44,
47–9
plaster 70, 71, 163, 185,
191
PREP formula 19
primary colour 32–3
primer 66

Radiators, painting 59
repetition 102, 105, 132
resources 219
restyling tips 8, 11, 84, 217
rooms, connecting 100–5,
204–15
by repetition 102, 105,
132
with colour 19, 30, 35, 56,
100, 104, 139
Rowland, Daniel & Nina 19,
46, 50, 71, 74, 102, 132,
163, 169, 185, 197, 218
rugs 106, 147, 150, 163–4,
219

Seating
dining areas 147, 148, 151
home office 200
living room 157, 164
upholstery 53, 77, 164
second hand items 74,
76–7, 136, 164, 176, 178,
219
secondary colour 32–3
shelves
bedroom 96, 97
dining areas 148, 152–3
kitchen 118–20, 131, 140
niches 99, 182, 184
styling basics 37–49
shoes, storage 11, 208
sinks 142–3, 182, 184, 191,
194
slow decorating 159,
190–1, 217
smartphone 8, 14, 15, 50,
51
sofa 53, 77, 161, 163–4,

166, 169
staircases 205, 210–15
stone
flooring 87, 88
worktops 140
storage 96–9
bathroom 182, 191
bedroom 96, 175, 177
dining area 148
entrance/hallway 207–8,
213
living area 159
planning 19
styling
basics 8, 37–53
choosing opposites 131
future-proofing 84
getting started 8
hidden details 108–10
suppliers 219

Tables, dining 147
taps 142–3, 191
television 108–9, 159, 169,
171
texture
bathrooms 192–3
connecting rooms 100
neutral schemes 74, 164
planning stage 22, 28,
217
shelving displays 46
walls 71, 163
tiles
bathroom 186–7
floor 87, 88, 139, 207, 213
splashbacks 125, 135,
137
treasures
displaying 118, 208, 217
as inspiration 15, 22, 34,
35
styling basics 42, 44, 56

Undercoat 66
upholstery 53, 77
UPVC, painting 72
utility room 208

Vignettes, creating 49,
50–2

vintage items
bathroom 182, 191
bedroom 176, 178
buying/treating 77, 219
connecting rooms 100
home office 202
as inspiration 34
kitchen 120, 124–6, 136
Vos, Ivo see Cutts, Jessie

Wall hangings 83
wallpaper 74, 100, 102,
131, 194, 195, 214, 219
walls
choosing opposites 131
connecting rooms 102,
105
lighting 90
paint 66, 68, 69, 160
plaster 70–1, 163, 185,
191
texture 71, 74
wardrobes, fitted 96
Wengraf, Guy & Kitty 131,
166, 179, 186, 200, 203,
207, 218
wetrooms 182
wheelchairs 84, 135
windows
double-glazing 84
trim colour 58–9, 72, 131
window seat 148
wood
bathrooms 195
de-oranging 77
dining areas 148
flooring 87, 88
kitchen 130–1, 132–3,
136
paint 66
staircase 213, 214
stripped 70, 76
worktops 140–3

Zoning 106, 147, 148–55

About the author

Lucy Gough is an interior stylist and art director for leading interiors brands and lifestyle magazines, as well as an online course creator and lecturer.

Lucy's work has appeared in many interior magazines in the UK and Australia, including *Livingetc, Homes & Gardens, YOU magazine, The Sunday Times, House Beautiful UK* (where she had a 'design your space column'), *Jones* magazine and *Country Homes & Interiors*. She has also worked for many leading brands, including John Lewis, Marks & Spencer, Dulux, Crown Paint and The Iconic (and so many more).

After teaching the Interior Styling short course at the University of the Arts (UAL) in London's Kings Cross, Lucy launched an online course 'How to Become a Professional Interior Stylist'. Soon afterwards came a second course 'How to Style Your Home Like a Magazine'. Lucy now has well over 1,600 students. All have left 5-star reviews. Additional online courses are added to Lucy's platform regularly.

Delivering workshops to groups of interiors enthusiasts and professionals is a particular favourite activity of Lucy's. These include events for Heal's and *Livingetc*, as well as teaching online interiors workshops on the Times+ platform.

Lucy currently lives between London and Sydney with her wife Kristina and two children, Arthur and Hamish.

Visit
lucygoughstylist.com
IG @style_by_lucy

About the Photographer
Simon Bevan is a leading interior and lifestyle photographer based in London. His work has been featured globally for both editorial and commercial campaigns, including for *Dezeen, Goop, ELLE Decoration*, Georg Jensen, *GQ*, and many more.

Simon's passion for art and design, along with his ability to harness and capture light in every image, is one of the many things that makes him among the most in-demand photographers in the UK and beyond.

Lucy and Simon have been working together for the last decade, collaborating on numerous magazine and commercial shoots, and they always strive to add a little bit of magic to every image they create.

Visit
simonbevan.com
IG @sibev

Author's acknowledgments

To be sitting here writing a dedication page for my own book is a lifelong dream come true. It wouldn't have been possible without my wonderful Publisher Alison Starling who approached me to write this handbook and then stood by me the whole way, patiently answering my many questions, and helped guide me through the whole process. I cannot thank you enough, truly.

To Jonathan Christie, Octopus's brilliant Creative Director, for turning an unimpressive word document into the beautiful hardcover book you are holding today. A big thank-you also goes to the wider Octopus team for all the bits that have happened in between, including Sybella Stephens for making sure my words read with clarity, Caroline West for beautifully copy editing and Emily Noto for going to so much trouble on the production side. It's been a privilege to collaborate with you all.

In my world, styling is only ever half the job. The other half goes to my wonderful friend and photographer of this book, Simon Bevan. It's always an absolute joy to work with you; this book was no exception. Simon, promise me we will always have a laugh-a-minute!

Ian (@iantillotson), I loved spending two weeks with you on set. Thank you for being Simon's right-hand guy and helping us achieve the incredible number of shots we created for these pages.

Kasia (@dwell_nicely), thank you for being a superstar and helping to pull all the mood boards together in the pre-shoot stage. Your attention to detail is impeccable, and your smile is always so sparkly.

Thank you to all the wonderful people who opened their homes to Simon and me. I loved spending time with you and getting to know you. It was memory-making at its absolute best.

To the fabulous location agencies Location Guys, Light Locations, PeaGreen and Lordship Park, who helped me find a number of the beautiful homes in this book – thank you for helping me start this journey in the very beginning.

To all the students on my online courses, thank you for believing in me as a teacher and for being part of a wonderful and supportive community.

To my beautiful friends and family. Thank you for being my cheer squad – you know who you are! x

Thank you to my beautiful sister Emma and my Mum for being my sounding board for this book and so many of my life decisions. You will never know how much you mean to me. Here's to many more Angel moments together. And to my Dad for just being you. You always make me laugh, and I hope you never stop telling stories. If you actually started writing them down, you would rival Roald Dahl, for sure!

To my beautiful boys Arthur and Hamish. I don't know what I did to deserve you, but you take my breath away every day. Never stop creating things. You both have the most amazing imaginations and have taught me so much in your few years on this planet. I am excited to watch you grow into the kind, handsome, strapping lads I know you will be.

I have to leave the most important dedication until last. To my incredible wife Kristina for being the person I thought only existed in fairy tales. Meeting you took my life in a direction I could never have imagined – we are a dream team. Thank you for keeping my head above water this year and for always championing me. I'm so proud to be your wife. ILUSM.

If you love this book, explore my online courses: courses.lucygoughstylist.com

All my videos, presentations and tasks are pre-recorded so I can teach you in your own time right from your sofa. All you need is a laptop, tablet or phone – nothing else. You can enrol and start learning instantly.

Lucy x

An Hachette UK Company
www.hachette.co.uk

First published in Great Britain in
2023 by Mitchell Beazley,
a division of Octopus Publishing
Group Ltd,
Carmelite House,
50 Victoria Embankment,
London EC4Y 0DZ
www.octopusbooks.co.uk
www.octopusbooksusa.com

Distributed in the US by
Hachette Book Group
1290 Avenue of the Americas
4th and 5th Floors
New York, NY 10104

Distributed in Canada by
Canadian Manda Group
664 Annette St.
Toronto, Ontario,
Canada M6S 2C8

ISBN 978 1 78472 863 2

A CIP catalogue record for
this book is available from the
British Library.

Printed and bound in China

10 9 8 7 6 5 4

Text by Lucy Gough
Photography by Simon Bevan

Publisher: Alison Starling
Creative Director: Jonathan Christie
Senior Managing Editor:
 Sybella Stephens
Copy Editor: Caroline West
Assistant Production Manager:
 Emily Noto

Picture credits
Page 7, portrait by Rekha Damhar @
picturerex_rekhadamha.
Page 14 above left, Beto Galetto/
Unsplash.
Page 14 below, Fulvio Ambrosanio/
Unsplash.
Page 62 right, Christina Deravedisian/
Unsplash.
Pages 80 and 158, artwork in
photograph © Judy Martin/Copyright
Agency. Licensed by DACS 2023.
Page 128 below left, Ilnur Kalimullin/
Unsplash.
Page 128 below right, Janine Meuche/
Unsplash